This is for you,
Miss Olive Rose

the crafty kid

kelly doust

MURDOCH BOOKS

Foreword

In the outdoor laundry at my grandmother's house stood rows and rows of wooden shelves that seemed to groan and bend under the weight of bottled preserves and plump homemade treats all year round.

Fat purple plums sat in thick syrup, alongside jars of sweet jams and spicy chutneys. There were preserved peaches that smelled of summer and bottles of homemade tomato sauce lined the walls like tall, red soldiers.

As Nana toiled with the old hand-wringer washing machine, grating pure Sunlight soap into the warm water, I would survey our stores with pride.

Nothing at my grandmother's house went to waste. Along with this plentiful produce from the garden, old magazines, greeting cards, buttons, ribbons and remnants were all recycled and put to good use once again. Even petals from the flower beds would be gathered up along with cloves and cinnamon sticks to become fragrant baskets of potpourri.

My favourite toy began life as one of Nana's fur coats. Stuffed with soft webbing and sewn into the shape of a dog, he had button eyes that didn't match and a black knitted nose. His fabulous floppy ears were made from the velvet collar of one of my sister's old dresses. Nothing ever looked, smelled or felt like him and I loved him all the more because he was homemade.

Like generations before her, my grandmother knew how to make things last – and to savour the joy of creating things by hand. But by the time I grew up, sadly, I must admit that I'd managed to master almost none of her thrifty skills. Sure, I do justice to some of her recipes, I can knit a little and sew on a button, but the truth is I'm just not crafty. Or patient. For me, a stitch in time usually means having to start all over again.

So, you can imagine how relieved and grateful I was when I discovered Kelly Doust's *The Crafty Minx*.

Like my grandmother, Kelly has been scouring flea markets and hoarding 'useful little things' since she was a girl. Her talent in transforming these into a myriad of practical treasures and funky fashions takes me back to a time when life was simple and passed by gently. To a time when a certain inner peace and meditative quality could be found in the domestic arts, and when precious little was deemed 'disposable'.

Kelly inspires us to rediscover the joy of creating and reinventing things just like our grandmothers did. Whether you're a crafty type or not, the projects in this book are so satisfyingly simple that you'll find yourself making gifts and much loved keepsakes for years to come.

And in the quiet, meditative rhythm of your happy crafting, perhaps you will find you've picked up a thread from another era and managed to weave its magic into your own.

– Joanna Webber, Associate Editor, *Australian Women's Weekly*

contents

Creating a Crafty Kid

The thing I love most about being creative is the feeling I get from it. It's such a wonderful occurrence, to be lost in the making of something. It channels the energy. Voracious readers know a similar kind of escapism well (sensing the world and all its concerns recede while you focus on the story at hand) but the nicest aspect about creating in your spare time is that you have some lovely object to show for it at the end.

Whether making something for yourself or another person, crafting is a little like placing the moment on pause and capturing the way you felt with this physical thing you've made. It makes no difference if the idea is your own or if you're following a pattern, because you chose to create that very thing right in the moment. And when you share it with others, it becomes the beginning of a conversation. How about that? Craft as dialogue.

This brings me to the other thing I love about creativity and crafting in general – it engenders community. At least, the kind of community I want to engage with more and more these days.

When I wrote my first book, *The Crafty Minx*, a number of friends asked me to host craft afternoons with their children. So one very wet Saturday, my treasured friend Catherine came around with her two kids, Jamie and Lucy, for the first of these. Arriving on my doorstep with an orange blossom cake still hot from the oven (Catherine is a domestic goddess of the baking variety) and shaking rain from their heads, they piled into our tiny kitchen and set to work, to the tune of a hailstorm battering the tin roof outside. We collectively came up with the idea to create the Kitchen lovebirds mobile included in this book and made it together (turn to page 25 for instructions to make your own), so there you can see just one of the things we achieved that afternoon.

You know how so often we experience something but it's not until afterwards we realise quite how special it was? Either the activity, or the time, or just the people we were with? That day was a bit like that. Catherine rang me a few days later to say thank you. She told me that when she was tucking Jamie into bed that night, he'd said, 'Mum, that was the best day I've had in ages.' And you know what? It was for me too – and I've had some pretty good days lately. It was just so enjoyable to be with my gorgeous friend, her seriously delightful, polite kids and to catch up on each other's news over bits of fabric and ribbon and wire, scoffing delicious cake slathered in lavender cream and drinking copious cups of Monk Pear tea. And I will never look at my mobile again, suspended in the middle of our kitchen window, without revisiting it. The many afternoons I've had crafting with friends since have been more or less the same.

This warm, downright wholesome feeling is pretty much the polar opposite of how I feel after watching downright trashy TV, reading a gossip magazine or eating too many sweets (activities I do like to indulge in sometimes). I think it's because the things I've mentioned are all fairly hollow pleasures, and being creative is a much more satisfying activity, along the lines of watching a decent film or documentary, reading good literature or indulging in a beautifully prepared, healthy meal instead. In solitude, crafting has given me huge reserves of quiet contentment and in company, made me feel a great deal of pleasure and connection with other people. In short, the main skills (and it is a skill, being able to generate these feelings within ourselves) that I want to pass on to my own children.

When I was very young, I would spend hours – days, even – making things and writing stories. It seemed like I always had a project on the go, especially over the long school holidays. It gave me such a huge sense of achievement to finish something, and a (quite possibly, over-confident) feeling that no-one had a perspective quite like me. I really believed I could do anything or be anyone I wanted, even in the stasis of childhood. It made me quite impatient to grow up and get started!

When I hit my late teens and finished school, travel, going out and work became my new passions. I loved eating out and being entertained in my spare time, and all but forgot about my interest in writing and making things, mainly because I spent so little time at home. Apart from customising clothes and the odd bit of furniture, I didn't really make anything for years, and worked increasingly hard in a career that felt a bit like a rat race. What's that saying? Even if you win, at the end of it all you're still a rat. I felt a little like that.

Then about five years ago, I met my dear friend Maggie, who urged me to start being creative again. With encouragement, I re-connected with those earlier feelings I used to have when I fed my creative life. I remembered the importance of sitting still for once, and began to remember what it was like to think in that rich sub-text that transforms everyday, mundane tasks into something special. Soon the ideas started flowing about what I could do to make my external life once again resemble more closely the inner workings of my imagination, as it had all those years ago when I was a child.

At first I took baby steps. My creative muscle had withered away from lack of use and it took a while before I would find a way to comfortably flex it again. I tentatively wrote a story here and made something kooky there. I fashioned things by hand for home and friends, approaching editors with ideas and composing the occasional freelance piece for a magazine – offering to work for free for the opportunity to be published. I contributed stories to a couple of collections, gave away quirky toys and handbags, and lost my anxiety about what people would think. I felt happier than I had in years.

Happiness is fleeting, coming in and out of our lives at different times, but I know that I've finally found a recipe for sidling up as close as possible to it each day. And making things for my daughter, and the people I care about, has been more rewarding than any of my other so-called accomplishments.

This is why I think it's so important for all of us to indulge our creative sides and teach our children to do the same. Also to find a way to get our creative output 'out there' and appreciated by other people. We humans are social beings after all, and thrive on feedback and encouragement. We particularly thrive on feeling a connection with others. Without it, I'm convinced something important withers and dies inside us. Turning your creative passions into a reality or even, amazingly, your livelihood, will feed your soul in the healthiest way. And receiving recognition for it is an entirely positive way to receive attention – not an insignificant point in our current culture of rampant celebrity, or fame for fame's sake.

Finding the time to be creative isn't always easy. Finding the time to teach your children to do so is even harder. It requires patience, and empty hours in which to practise it. A long weekend with few commitments is best, even though they don't come around often. But the rewards are high, because nurturing creativity is just as important as nurturing intelligence in children. You'll be teaching them a self-sufficiency that is all but lost to many people. And you'll be passing on skills they will carry with them for the rest of their lives.

I have ordered the projects in this book to give you inspiration for feeding each aspect of your child's life, starting with ideas for making fun things for the kitchen and ending with altogether more soothing items for their bedrooms. The projects should be pleasing to make but also, in the main, useful. And if nothing else, they make wonderful last-minute gifts because they are so quick and easy to complete.

Here's a call to all Crafty Minxes: start your children crafting young, and encourage them to keep at it. They may or may not end up pursuing it, but they'll always have craft as a hobby; something to occupy, feed and enrich them indefinitely. This can only be A Good Thing. Don't be nostalgic for a time when we made more things for and with our children – simply start now in your own home. It's such a simple and satisfying way to entertain them, and doesn't require much of a budget.

Playing with crafts also encourages us to spend more quality time with the children in our lives, and I'm sure we could all do with a bit more of that.

Someday, crafts might again become a major part of the developed world, less like a fashionable (re)discovery so many of us post-feminist, post-post-modern (or is that three posts now? I'm not sure) women have found (which may, like all fashions, pass) and more a constant, evolving, necessary aspect of our daily lives. Wouldn't that be lovely?

Why make your treasures from recycled materials?

Being the eldest child and the only girl of three, I've never had that built-in aversion to hand-me-downs that so many children, born subsequently in families, have. I actually adored being given second-hand clothes on the few occasions they came my way. I thought they helped me convey a certain womanly sophistication I did not feel (based on the assumption that the previous wearer did). Although I've largely grown out of such gawky, teenage awkwardness, I still feel buoyed by the sartorial elegance of earlier times when I wear vintage and pre-loved clothes.

But simply re-using worn clothes in the way they were intended is not always possible – or desirable. To paraphrase a popular saying, we often hurt the ones we love most (true as well, sadly, with our favourite things) and sometimes fashion dictates that a certain look will not be popular again… at least not for many years, and who can bear to hold on to them, taking up valuable wardrobe space, until then?

One of the many credos I try to live by is this: if you don't love it or use it, get rid of it (or, preferably, don't buy it in the first place). My friend's mother once suggested this and it's been one of the best pieces of advice I've ever received. Refashioning old clothes and belongings into something new has to be the answer.

Even better: mixing them with new fabrics and materials will give your creations a modern edge, coolly informed by past and current ideas of hip.

I'm all about the 'high and low' – thrifty and vintage finds paired with covetable pieces from the new season; whether it be fabric, clothes, accessories or homewares. Wearing head-to-toe vintage can make you feel a bit like Second-hand Rose. Similarly, decking out your home in finds plucked exclusively from other eras conveys the notion you'd rather live in the past. But mixing everything up with an ample dash of *chutzpah* definitely shows you're in the know. It's very much the way forward.

By crafting, I also love to think that we can rescue things from landfill and do our very small bit to help the environment. Not to mention find ways to recycle innovatively in the face of an overly consumerist culture. A culture which is becoming increasingly (and disturbingly) homogenous. That's why there are so many practical tips for creating beautiful handmade items for kids from discarded materials in this book. I hope it offers people of all ages and with no background in crafts the confidence to look at their pre-loved belongings in a different way, with an eye to reinventing them. And if we lead by example ourselves, I'm sure we can pass on the old *make do and mend* adage to the next generation.

So go forth and craftily recycle, and enjoy things with a bit of history to them while you still can. Long live the Crafty Minx, and all hail the new generation of Crafty Kids. Hip hip hooray!

Kelly Doust

Getting started

Where to begin?

Before you read the following pages and allow yourself to get a little overwhelmed, please remember this: you don't actually need everything listed here, but much of it will come in handy if you want to reinvent yourself as a home crafter and all round chic Miss Suzy Homemaker. And because you'll be making things both for and with the kiddiewinks, there'll be lots of opportunities for the following items to earn their keep over the coming years.

Even if you don't have children, there are always birthdays and special occasions to make gifts for. With a cleverly-stocked crafts cupboard, the opportunity to do so – even at a moment's notice – will be at your fingertips.

I've included each piece of equipment on this list because I've found it useful myself, but have actually been quite slow to acquire everything in my own, reasonably modest collection. I don't have the space to keep much more, for a start, but I also like to keep things nicely ordered, so as not to forget I already own them and head off to the shops to purchase them again (which, let's face it, happens). Take your time when building up your equipment and supplies stash; there's no rush. Think of it as a journey rather than a destination.

Useful (but not essential) equipment for the crafts cupboard

✳ Tape measure

✳ Tracing paper

✳ Bobble-headed pins

✳ Sewing needles

✳ Larger embroidery/tapestry needles

✳ Dressmaking scissors (these are important: as with a cook's knife, buy the best you can afford)

✳ Small, sharp scissors for loose threads

✳ Pinking shears (scissors with a zigzag edge: not necessary, but good for cutting fabrics that fray easily, such as canvas, linen or wool)

✳ Dressmaker's chalk

✳ Quick unpick/seam ripper

✳ Sewing machine

✳ Standard machine needles

✳ Denim machine needles

✳ Bobbins and bobbin case

✳ Separate bobbin winder (you don't need this because you can wind bobbins on your machine, but they come in handy when you're using your machine a lot)

Rainy afternoon arts supplies

I do think everyone should stock a basic collection of art supplies in their home, perfect for whiling away those wet weekends with little ones or making your own party decorations. And it's far better than slouching about in front of the TV or computer, *non*?

Here are some suggestions for basic arts materials to get you started. Go on, you know you want to:

✳ Sketchbook – for drawing, jotting down ideas and creating a scrapbook of inspiring images

✳ A few artist's canvases in different shapes and sizes

✳ Staple gun and staples (good for making your own canvases or showing off clever fabric collages). These are inexpensive and useful for simple upholstery projects as well.

✳ Cardboard

✳ Acrylic paints – primary colours of blue, yellow, red, as well as white and black, mean you can mix any other colour you need

✳ Watercolours

✳ Paintbrushes in a variety of sizes

✳ Paper glue

✳ Paper scissors

A world of wonderful extras…
fabulous fabrics and materials for wee ones

J'adore natural fibres. Even though children can be less discerning, I think their soft and often sensitive skin calls for as many natural fabrics to be used as possible. But it's tricky, because you still need them to be hardy enough to withstand the spills, soakings and washes that are part and parcel of everyday life with children. Synthetics or synthetic mixes are much better for that sort of thing, but are just too nasty for my tastes… I'd rather wash by hand than make the sacrifice.

I've actually found that the thing which has most improved my life in this respect recently is a new washing machine. With a brilliant wool and delicates cycle, and a great soak setting so I don't forget things sitting in buckets of bleach for days (no doubt quietly disintegrating), I can now wash everything in the machine rather than by hand. I'm careful not to use harsh detergents for delicate things, only wool wash or soap flakes, and I always use fabric softener (except on denim jeans, when I want them to stay, ahem… supportive). It's certainly saved me a lot of time and effort – *très* important when you're a working mum (or anyone who values their spare time, and isn't that all of us, really?) I know it's a huge investment, but worth looking into if you struggle to keep on top of the washing basket and want your clothes to last longer.

Try to recognise the fabrics used all around you, and don't be afraid to rub your fingers against them to get a feel for their unique texture and suitability for different items – it's the only way to develop a sense of what's decent, and what's not. My favourite fabrics are still cotton, wool, linen and denim – even when it comes to making things for and with children. I will always love silk but it's just too high-maintenance to wear every day now I'm a mum, and especially too delicate for little people. I save my considerable collection of pre-baby silk frocks for nights out with friends, or dinner *à deux* with my husband, to avoid sticky little fingers.

As with cotton or denim, linen is surprisingly hard-wearing, but it does need a good iron almost every time it's washed, and I hate ironing more than almost any other household chore. I literally feel like my life's being sucked away while I do it, so I make an effort not to buy things that need a lot of ironing unless I absolutely adore them. That said, napkins, tablecloths or things in linen that are similarly simple to iron look magic. Crisp, clean and gorgeous.

Wool needs a bit of extra care in the washing department, but I don't really understand how you can clothe yourself or your kids in anything else in the cooler months. Fleece is fine, but just too ugly and ball-y after it's been in the wash even once, and those horrid puffa jackets have the effect of making anyone look like the Michelin man. Nothing else seems to seal the heat in or make you feel quite as warm and cosy as wool (and especially cashmere) in winter. And wool felt is just delicious to experiment with and for making cute toys and accessories.

Apart from pure wool felt, when it comes to children, the ultimate fabric has to be oilcloth. Not for clothing, but for the aprons, tablecloths, bags and myriad other things that need wiping down on a daily basis when little people join the family.

*Tip

Remember to always be on the hunt for good fabric, whether it's new or second-hand. Many of the most stylish printmakers and upholstery fabric suppliers sell remnants, ranging from tiny scraps to a few metres long, and a good way to get the most out of their distinctive patterns and high-quality finish is to mix them with less expensive materials such as denim, canvas or calico for the same upmarket look. Creative patchworking with small pieces also looks great and you should be able to find a use for even the smallest remnants.

Here are some useful materials to keep in mind when shopping for kids' projects:

* A selection of threads – black, white and beige are your essentials, but it's good to build up a whole rainbow of colours for use on all fabrics. The general rule is to match thread to your fabric (cotton for cotton, silk for silk and polyester/cotton for synthetics) but polyester/cotton threads are sturdy and work well on most fabrics. Colour-wise, anything goes: use a contrasting colour if you want to highlight hems, or a shade darker than your fabric if you want it to blend in. Another good tip is to wind half of your bobbins with basic colours at the same time, so they're ready when you need them

* Embroidery thread, also in a range of colours – red, white, black and pale blue are a good start for lovely contrasts but again, build up a rainbow as you go

* Delicious balls of wool in soft, bright and crazy colours

* Cross-stitch fabric (this can be an even-weave fabric, such as linen, or special cross-stitch fabric called Aida)

* Fabrics of every colour, pattern, texture and weave under the sun

* Wool felt in candy colours – online, Etsy has the best selection of hand-dyed felt I've found if you don't have the patience for dyeing it yourself

* Oilcloth – there is such a wonderful selection available online; go on and Google it!

* Calico

* Ribbons – grosgrain and velvet are my particular favourites

* Buttons – I buy almost all of mine at flea markets and charity stores. New buttons are so pricey!

* Rickrack

* Bias binding, especially the thicker kind – these days you can find a gorgeous selection decorated with stripes, polka dots and super-bright florals

* Interfacing

* Polyester fibrefill or wool stuffing

On the loose in the kitchen

Let's start in the kitchen, because it's the heart of any family home, and one of the best places for kids to really be creative and enjoy themselves. It's also the best place to teach them the simple pleasures of food and family time, and is my favourite room for these reasons.

Not rarely do I count myself lucky for having a reasonably healthy attitude towards food. I've always eaten a wide range of foods, and apart from a gluttonous blip when I first moved out of home and during University, very little of the processed or junky variety. I'm grateful for the fact that my 'comfort' staples are porridge, pasta and fruit rather than deep-fried chips, burgers or chocolate. It's only the cheese addiction I (sometimes) wish I could kick.

Over the years, I've had friends who have battled through eating disorders or craved rubbishy foods. Friends who skip meals because they're worried about getting fat. It seems obvious to me, that if you eat well and regularly, your body will work the way it's meant to. This is something I've learned that I'd like to pass on as a recipe for a healthy – and hopefully long – life.

That said, I'm no food Nazi. Denying yourself treats every once in a while tends to leach all the fun out of life. Being good 100% of the time is very boring: *everything in moderation.*

Food is a great leveller. It's also a form of communication for things we don't always say. Like how much we love someone, or want to be in their presence. A shared meal is a shared experience and although we don't remember every one, we often think about the enjoyable meals spent with people we care about, for many years on.

Moreover, the kitchen is a hub of creativity in the home. Not everyone has an affinity with, or talent for, food preparation but thankfully, there are so many simple meals to prepare (not necessarily from scratch), that everyone can feel a sense of achievement making and serving them. It's this sense of achievement that inspires us to experiment further, and grow bold. Preparing food should be fun rather than a chore, and if you believe (as I do) that food is medicine, you realise that every mouthful counts. Never is this more true than when nourishing children. They are watching you for cues on how to be. By having a healthy relationship with food you'll be giving them an early gift they will appreciate (and thank you for) later.

Cooking... with gas!

I love that cooking stores now seem to stock so many utensils and accessories for children. Letting them help you prepare food for the family is a great pastime, and before long you'll begin to reap the rewards of their experimentation.

Don't stress about mess – everything in the kitchen should be easy to clean or wipe down, anyway – as little fingers need to explore the brave new world of taste and texture that food offers. Keep an eye on them to make sure they're safe, but realise they need to make their own mistakes.

Start with something easy, like a cake – they can stir all the ingredients together AND lick the bowl – before letting them graduate to more ambitious projects involving knives, food processors and the oven. These could be introduced slowly, and offered as a reward for responsible behaviour.

Kitchen lovebirds mobile

I'm no twitcher, but I love birds – particularly the smaller kinds, like finches and hummingbirds. Seeing them in a cage just makes me too sad.

In Hong Kong, the tradition of *feng shui* considers it good luck to have a couple of caged birds in your office, or goldfish in a bowl; apparently they attract positive energy and wealth to the work environment. When I lived there, I worked in an office with cages and bowls both dotted about the office aplenty, and while it was nice to be distracted watching them from my cubicle, it also felt cruel leaving them there overnight; not even in a home where they could be loved and admired as part of the family.

We (me, my friend Catherine and her children, Jamie and Lucy) invented this mobile by committee during a crafternoon one wet weekend. This is a lovely project to make with children as it's uncomplicated and can easily be completed in an hour or two. The one on the right of the photo is Jamie's handiwork – I think I prefer it to my own with its characterful, wonky seams. It has such charm, don't you think?

Make a couple of your own pet birds for the heart of the home, and maybe you'll fool the feng shui gods into making every meal a success...

You will need

✳ One wire coathanger

✳ Tin snips

✳ Masking tape

✳ 2 m (2¼ yd) ribbon (this is more than enough)

✳ Sewing needle and thread

✳ Scraps of plain fabric: hemp or linen works quite well

✳ Scraps of patterned fabric: vintage, floral sprigs and brights look particularly lovely against the plain

✳ Embroidery thread – a few different shades work well

✳ Four small buttons (non-matching is fine)

✳ A very small amount of polyester fibrefill or fabric scraps to plump out your birds

✳ Chopstick

Instructions

1. Take your wire coathanger and cut off the hook and twisted part of its base with the tin snips. (If you're making this with a child, it's probably best to do this part yourself.)

2. Bend the wire into a rough heart shape, with a few centimetres (an inch) or so overlap on one of the sides of the heart.

3. Use a small amount of masking tape to bind the wire ends together.

4. Use another small piece of masking tape to hold down one end of your length of ribbon, then start winding the ribbon around the wire until you reach the end. I've suggested having a little extra ribbon just in case – you don't want to run out just before you reach the end.

5. Use your needle and thread to pop a few stitches in the ribbon when you've finished covering the entire wire heart shape, snipping off any excess ribbon.

6. Now take your small scraps of hemp and cut out a bird shape, as shown on page 230. Use the first cut-out piece of fabric as a pattern to make another three shapes the same size, taking care to make two pieces mirror-images of the first two.

7. Cut another two pairs of the smaller bird shapes from your small scraps of patterned fabric (four different pieces will look lovely, as long as they roughly match or look good together) to sit inside the hemp bird shape. They don't need to be perfect – an approximation of the shape will do.

8. Attach the patterned fabric to the outside of the hemp with a running stitch in a lovely bright embroidery thread, and sew on the button where the eye would be.

9. Repeat Step 8 until all four sides of the two birds are completed.

10. With the patterned fabric facing outwards, sew two mirror-image bird shapes together around the edges using an overcasting stitch – don't fret if it looks a little frayed and messy; that's its charm – and leave about 2.5 cm (1 in) open.

11. Use your chopstick to stuff the bird with a little polyfill or fabric scraps until it is plump, but not bursting at the seams.

12. Sew the open edge closed.

13. Repeat Steps 10–12 for the second bird.

14. Now thread a long length of embroidery cotton into your needle and make a small knot in the end of your thread.

15. Sew through the top part of the first bird, then through the ribbon on the wire, at the bottom corner of the heart.

16. When you're happy with the length of the thread hanging from the bottom of the heart, make a small knot.

17. Now sew through the bottom of the second bird, placing an extra stitch underneath so he stays put in the very centre of the heart shape.

18. Thread through the bird and place another stitch in the ribbon at the top of the heart. Make a small knot before ending the thread, also at the top. Use this to suspend it from a window frame or ceiling, simply knotting an extra length of cotton thread if it's not long enough. *Bellissima!*

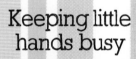

Keeping little hands busy

Encourage a child who can use scissors to help with cutting the bird shapes from scraps of fabric and sew around the edges. If they're a bit wonky, it will only add to the charm.

Smaller ones might like to glue pre-cut bird shapes onto cardstock for a pretty collage.

Mini-me aprons

These are the simplest aprons you will ever make, which means they're a perfect project for constructing with children. Create one for yourself, one to put away for a birthday gift and one for every member of the family while you're at it.

All the sewing can be done by hand and, with the right materials, you're already halfway there. Despite how easy this looks and is, indeed, easy to make, enjoy a warm glow of satisfaction when you're done. Who would have thought something so pretty could be made in two shakes of a lamb's tail?

Cooking is less of a chore when you have the cutest accessories…

You will need

This amount of oilcloth will make an apron to fit a child aged up to about 5 years. Adjust the measurements for a smaller or larger child.

* 35 cm wide × 45 cm high (14 × 18 in) oilcloth

* Ruler and pen

* Scissors

* About 2 m × 25 mm-wide (2¹/₄ yd × 1 in) bias binding

* Embroidery thread in 2 colours: one to match bias binding, one in a contrasting colour

* Embroidery needle

* 2 m (2¹/₄ yd) ribbon

Instructions

1. Take your rectangle of oilcloth, ruler and pen. Measure and make a small mark 10 cm (4 in) in from the top right-hand corner of the oilcloth, and 15 cm (6 in) down. Join the marks to make a rectangle in the corner.

2. Following the diagram (on page 237), sketch a smooth curve into the corner rectangle, as shown.

3. Use your scissors to cut away the excess fabric beyond the traced line.

4. Fold the rectangle in half lengthwise, right sides together, and trace the curved line onto the opposite upper corner – this will give you curves that match exactly. Cut along the traced line.

5. Take your bias binding and the apron-shaped oilcloth, and fold the binding over the edge of the bottom left-hand corner. Secure in place with a couple of small, firm stitches, then use a running stitch in matching embroidery thread to fix the bias binding around the entire border.

6. When you reach a corner, fold the bias binding under itself into a neat corner and keep stitching. You might want to insert another stitch diagonally (just to be safe) at each corner.

7. When you get back to the beginning, leave a little extra and chop off any excess binding. Fold raw end underneath at an angle and stitch firmly in place.

8. Cut a 50 cm (20 in) length of ribbon and cut the remaining ribbon into two equal pieces. Place one end of the 50 cm (20 in) length of ribbon under the top right-hand corner of the apron, at the back. Use your contrasting embroidery thread and needle to fix the strap in place with three small, x-shaped stitches.

9. Close the loop by securing the other side in place as well.

10. Secure the remaining lengths of ribbon to either corner at the sides, using the same 'x' stitches. Yee-hah, you've got yourself an apron, pardner!

Petite pot holders

Little people need to learn what they can and can't touch in the kitchen, particularly when it comes to the dangers of a hot plate or stove. But by teaching them this while they're young, and charging them with the responsibility to treat its dangers with respect, you'll give them confidence in the kitchen for life.

Here's a set of pot holders for culinarily inclined children. Encourage kids to use them whenever they're around hot plates or for grabbing hot-handled pots and pans from the stove. Adults will find them useful as well, even made to the same dimensions.

Choose a bright and playful fabric, such as this very hardy 100% cotton striped deckchair material, bought as a remnant from an upholsterer, to appeal to your child's sense of fun.

You will need

* 50 × 20 cm (20 × 8 in) sturdy, 100% natural fabric: deckchair fabric is ideal but any strong upholstery material will work

* The same amount from an old towel, to be used as wadding

* Ruler

* Dressmaker's chalk

* Scissors

* Approximately 1 m × 25 mm-wide (39 in × 1 in) bias binding

* Sewing machine and thread to match your bias binding

* Denim needle

Instructions

1. Lay your canvas strip out flat, wrong side facing up, and lay the towelling strip on top. Fold the whole sandwich in half crosswise, so the canvas is enclosing the towelling.

2. Use a saucer or something similar to trace a curved edge onto the corners opposite the fold and cut along your traced line through all layers. Use your machine to sew a line of stitching around the outside to keep all four layers in place.

3. Take your ruler and chalk and use them to draw a cross in the middle of the fabric, stretching from corners to curved edges.

4. Measure further lines stretching out from this centre cross at 4 cm (1^1/$_2$ in) intervals to give a criss-crossed diamond effect.

5. Sew lines of stitching over this grid of diamonds, then dust or wipe away the original chalk lines with a damp cloth.

6. Take your bias binding and wrap it around the raw edge of the fabric, starting at the top left-hand corner.

7. Sew into place until all four edges are covered and you are back to the starting point, then keep sewing a further 10 cm (4 in) along the bias binding to create a little tail.

8. Chop off any excess bias binding and fold the raw edge of the tail under itself by a couple of millimetres (^{1}/$_4$ in).

9. Fold tail over on itself to create a loop and then sew into place at the corner.

10. Follow the above instructions to create a second pot holder, then go handle some hot things, taking care that all fingers and thumbs are covered by your super-cute pot holders.

The joy of Honey Joys

These were, hands down, my favourite treat when I was little. Not the most healthy, but certainly very scrummy. I remember gorging myself on them, and sometimes picking off each cornflake one by one to savour them all the longer. Cajole kids into completing the weekly chores by promising to make Honey Joys with them when they're done, and you'll have them begging you for more jobs to do (what a boon!).

Made simply from cornflakes, butter, sugar and honey, these are quicker and easier than baking biscuits, and will have the kids convinced they're master chefs. Pop them in pretty, rainbow-coloured cupcake cases, and watch them fly off the rack before they've even cooled.

*Make a large stack of these in one go –
they'll disappear more quickly than you think!*

You will need

* 3 cups cornflakes
* 50 g (1³/₄ oz) butter
* 1 tablespoon sugar
* 2 tablespoons honey
* Large cupcake cases
* Cupcake or muffin tray for 6–8 large Honey Joys

Instructions

1. Preheat your oven to 160°C (325°F).

2. Put the butter, sugar and honey into a saucepan or microwave-safe bowl and melt gently on the stove or in the microwave.

3. Add your 3 cups of cornflakes to the bowl or pan and mix well with a wooden spoon. Try not to crush up the cornflakes too much.

4. Spoon the mixture into your cupcake cases and pop in the oven for 9 minutes.

5. When the timer goes off, remove Honey Joys from the oven, place on a wire rack to cool and leave to set for at least half an hour before scoffing.

Keeping little hands busy

Your little one should be able to help you measure the ingredients, gently mix them together in the bowl and spoon into the cupcake cases – just keep an eye on them near the oven.

Windowsill herb garden

I've always loved nurturing a few plants on my kitchen windowsill. Watering them with leftovers from a bedside glass or grey water from the sink couldn't be easier, and pests are easily disposed of at such close quarters without using any nasty sprays. Kids will get a kick out of watching them thrive, especially when you live in a flat or home without much space for a garden.

The nicest thing with herbs is you can incorporate them into your cooking as well, and they're cheap and easy to replace when they start looking a bit sad. We don't bother growing herbs from scratch: simply purchase them from a supermarket or greengrocer and re-pot in terracotta with good drainage and a saucer underneath.

Basil plants are my number one favourite for a sunny windowsill. They like lots of water and the more you pinch off the leaves, the better they seem to grow. Rinse and mix with cherry tomatoes and buffalo mozzarella for a delicious light lunch, drizzled with extra-virgin olive oil, balsamic vinegar and a pinch of salt and pepper.

Lemon thyme is another goodie, great for frying up with mushrooms or adding to simple pastas, salads and casseroles. Oregano is a winner for the same types of dishes, and a couple of freshly chopped chives will completely transform scrambled eggs on toast into an art form, or give risotto a wonderful *oomph* when thrown in right towards the end of cooking.

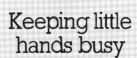

Keeping little hands busy

A child who can read and write could print the names of the herbs onto popsicle sticks so you know what's what as it grows. A younger tot might like to record the growth of seedlings by making daily marks on a thin bamboo stake.

You will need

* Pot of herbs, purchased from a local greengrocer or supermarket or grown from seeds if you're feeling ambitious

* Someone willing to be responsible for watering it

* A saucer or plate to catch run-off water

* A sunny spot on the kitchen counter or windowsill

Instructions

1. Find a pretty pot to hold your herbs.

2. Plant with a little extra potting mix.

3. Water daily or whenever the soil is looking dry.

4. Harvest for mealtimes, storing any leftovers in your fridge's crisp box.

*Tip

Herbs do not like to stand constantly in a saucer of water, so make sure, if you have to use a saucer under your pots to contain drips, that you are not over-watering. Alternatively, stand the pots on pebbles in your saucer. If your container has no drainage hole, use it to hold an inner pot.

Set the table!

My friend Maggie Hamilton, a social researcher, has gathered a lot of information to suggest that homes where people don't seem to talk much with their kids – mainly over shared meals – are beset more often with 'problem' tweens and teenagers suffering from self-esteem issues. Adults know how important it is to download their thoughts and feelings after a long day at work, so it's hardly surprising that it's just as important for children to share their feelings and experiences at the end of each day, and to know we are listening.

The dining table is a wonderful place to have conversations and stimulate discussion in any household. Food provides a welcome distraction when articulation fails us, but most importantly, we can just be with each other, picking up on the nuances of speech and behaviour that signal when something might be wrong. We won't always know when problems occur in our children's lives, but we'll have a far better chance at noticing if we spend more time like this together.

This is why I hope to make eating at the table non-negotiable in our house as our family grows – not necessarily every night, but more often than not. Even a half-hour shared meal can be an oasis of calm in our busy lives, and connect us face-to-face with those we care about most.

'Meet the family' tablecloth

There's not much new under the sun when it comes to crafts (or anything for that matter, don't you think?). I was ruminating on how to make suppertime more fun for children as well as wondering what I could do to recycle our lovely white (but unfortunately stained) damask tablecloth recently, when I came up with the idea for this. A few days later, I opened the latest issue of the super-inspiring French magazine, *marie claire idées*, to find something similar within. It's interesting to me that people from all over the place seem to come to creative conclusions at the same time.

Appliqué prettily-patterned 'plates' to a plain tablecloth, and stitch the names of family members above each place at the table as a paean to your favourite people. This is an especially nice idea for special occasions like Christmas dinner and birthday parties, and will make a nice addition to the linen cupboard for many years to come.

*Tip

This tablecloth makes a brilliant gift for any family. Why not make one for friends who've just had another child, or to celebrate a housewarming?

You will need

✴ Damask tablecloth or tablecloth-sized length of plain fabric

✴ Smaller pieces of contrasting fabric for the appliquéd plates

✴ Dinner plate

✴ Dressmaker's chalk

✴ Bobble-headed pins

✴ Sewing machine and thread

✴ Embroidery needle and thread in a variety of colours

Instructions

1. Lay the tablecloth over your dining table, with the edges falling neatly to roughly the same length at each corner.

2. Make sure the chairs are placed at evenly-spaced intervals around the table, as you'll be using the centre of each chair back as a guide to where your plates will go.

3. Lay your dinner plate on a piece of patterned fabric and use your dressmaker's chalk to trace around its circumference. Repeat this for each place setting required, that is, for each member of your family.

4. When you've cut out all your plates, pin them in their places on the tablecloth.

5. Set your machine to a small zigzag setting and then sew around the outside of the plates until all are fixed to the tablecloth, removing the pins as you go.

6. Lay the tablecloth down on the table again then use your dressmaker's chalk to write each person's name above his or her plate in a cursive handwriting.

7. Use the embroidery needle and thread to pick out the names in backstitch.

8. Lay the table and get ready to break bread. Amen.

'Here comes the plane' appliquéd napkins

Children can be remarkably stubborn when it comes to mealtimes. I remember very well the first few months of teaching our daughter to eat. I spent hours boiling, mashing and straining organic vegetables into a palatable mush, only to have them spat out and dribbled down her chin, dropped uneaten on the floor or flung at my hair and face. Anywhere but in her tummy, annoyingly. That's when I decided to give her supermarket-bought organic baby food instead until she began to co-operate a bit more... much less hassle.

Eventually, I found the tactic that worked best was encouragement: like most of us, Olive responds well to flattery and attention. I started telling her what a good girl she was after every mouthful, gave her lots of smiles and pretended to eat and enjoy her food myself. And yes, I tried 'Here comes the plane' (the things we do...) Touch wood, it's been blue skies ever since.

✳ Tip

Appliquéd items aren't necessarily more fragile (as you know, patches often strengthen things) but do need a bit of extra care in the wash. With clothes, turn appliquéd items inside-out, just in case, and if your appliqué patch is made of a different fabric to the piece it's attached to, you will still need to adhere to its particular washing instructions - that is, wool and felt will shrink if washed in hot water, and silk will go funny if you use harsh detergents or don't treat it as the delicate fibre it is.

You will need

For four napkins

❋ Four large squares of linen, approximately 50 cm (20 in): I've used a horribly cut 1980s sundress found in a charity store which I doubt had been worn. The linen was the perfect weight, feel and colour for napkins

❋ Dressmaker's scissors

❋ Ruler

❋ Soft pencil or dressmaker's chalk

❋ Iron

❋ Sewing machine and thread

❋ Assorted pieces of felt in light grey, dark grey, cream and red

❋ Small scissors

❋ Sewing needle and cotton thread to match felt

❋ Red embroidery thread

❋ Rickrack

Instructions

1. Lay your fabric out flat and, using the ruler and dressmaker's chalk, measure and cut four 50 cm (20 in) squares. It is important to cut your squares precisely on the straight grain of the fabric, so get your fabric squared up before you start cutting.

2. Take your first square and your iron, and press under 1 cm ($^3/8$ in) along each raw edge.

3. Open out the edges again and you will see you have pressed a tiny 1 cm ($^3/8$ in) square into each corner of the napkin. Use your ruler to rule a diagonal line across each corner of the napkin at the inner corner of this little square. Trim off the corner along your ruled line. This will reduce bulk on the finished napkin and keep the corners neat. Repeat for the three remaining corners of the napkin.

4. Now press under 1 cm ($^3/8$ in) again on each edge as before, then press under another 1 cm ($^3/8$ in) on each edge and pin or tack the hems in place.

5. Stitching close to the inner pressed edge of the hem, stitch along one side of the napkin right to the edge. Leaving the needle in the fabric, lift the presser foot and swivel the fabric around so that you are sewing at right angles to the previous line of stitching. Stitch a tiny square of stitching in the corner of the napkin to hold the corner of the hem in place, pivoting on each corner, until you have completed the square and are ready to sew the next side of the hem.

6. Repeat Step 5 for each corner of the napkin.

7. Repeat Steps 2–6 for each fabric square.

8. For the appliqué, take your felt and cut out the shapes (provided in the pattern template on page 231) for the plane.

9. Place the shapes on the edge of your napkin, as shown in the photograph, and start sewing into place using small running stitch and matching sewing thread.

10. Use the red embroidery thread and a long running stitch for the vapour trail.

11. Trim the edges of each napkin with rickrack.

Pretty felt & ribbon cutlery rolls

Not too long ago, I purchased a set of eight matching dessert forks and fruit knives from an antiques store. Dated at roughly a century-and-a-half old, they had managed to survive beautifully so far, treated with care. As they were already a little scratched and worn, I didn't want to add to the damage, so decided to make this cutlery roll to keep them safe. I bring them out for afternoon tea with friends or when sharing Portuguese tarts with the family for elevenses, and always wash by hand rather than in the dishwasher.

A cutlery roll is a good solution if you want to keep silverware from scratching in the drawer, but also works well for storing picnic cutlery or keeping sharp knives and bottle openers together when you're travelling. Make one out of protective felt to fit any set, and add a favourite ribbon to tie closed.

*Tip

Another very cute reason to make this felt & ribbon roll is for storing children's pencils and stationery. Simply make the gaps the right size for items you want to store, and pop pencils and bits and pieces inside the pockets before rolling up tight and closing with a bow.

Keeping little hands busy

Ask your child to help you put the cutlery into the finished pockets. If you are teaching a toddler to eat with utensils, why not make a special cutlery roll, pop in the pint-sized knife, fork and spoon and let them unwrap it themselves at each mealtime as part of the fun.

You will need

Adjust the measurements here to suit the size of your silverware if your pieces are larger or smaller.

* 28 × 28 cm (11 × 11 in) pretty cotton fabric

* 28 × 28 cm (11 × 11 in) felt

* 25 × 11 cm (10 × 4^1/$_2$ in) felt in a contrasting colour

* Ruler

* Dressmaker's pencil

* 60 cm (24 in) ribbon, cut into two lengths of 30 cm (12 in)

* Sewing machine and thread

Instructions

1. Place your larger piece of felt on the fabric square, right sides together, and sew around all four edges, allowing a 6 mm (^{1}/$_4$ in) seam and leaving a gap of about 5 cm (2 in).

2. Trim corners, turn right side out and press, then fold in the open edges and slipstitch closed.

3. Take your smaller piece of felt and measure 3.5 cm (1^1/$_2$ in) in from each short side. Rule a light line across the felt at these points.

4. Now divide the remaining space between the ruled lines into six equal vertical compartments and rule light lines across the felt at each point.

5. Place the smaller piece of felt over the larger piece along the bottom edge, with the end of one length of ribbon sandwiched between the two pieces on the right-hand edge.

6. Stitching 6 mm (^{1}/$_4$ in) from the edge, topstitch the felt rectangle into place along the outer three edges. Reverse a few times at either end for strength, and when you sew across the ribbon.

7. Sew along each line you have marked with the pencil as well, reverse stitching at either end.

8. Use a damp cloth to brush away the pencil marks and turn over to the other side.

9. Take the remaining piece of ribbon, fold under the raw end and stitch into place vertically, 10 cm (4 in) in from the left-hand edge (on the seam of one line of stitching).

10. Pop in your cutlery so it can get settled in its nice new home.

Divine egg cosies

Ah, my favourite hot breakfast: soft-boiled eggs and buttery soldiers. Is there anything more delicious on a cold winter's morning? (Porridge with strawberries, banana and honey, maybe.) I have such wonderful memories of eating these at the table as a child. There's nothing like that satisfying 'crack' as you lop the top off your egg, and the yolk pours out – only to be caught by its first soldier. How can you *not* love a googie egg?

Keep your eggs warm with a handmade felt cosy that looks cuter than pie on a plate. Children will love constructing this funny hat. Paired with an egg cup and chocolate egg, you also have a wonderful gift to give anyone of any age at Easter.

Go wild coming up with ideas to decorate your egg cosies with the kids and remember: anything goes

You will need

* Wool felt in a variety of colours

* Scissors

* Embroidery thread in a variety of colours

* Embroidery needle

* 5 cm (2 in) length of ribbon or cotton tape for each cosy

Instructions

1. Cut the cosy shape (on page 233) twice, from the felt you've decided to use for the main part of the cosy.

2. From a contrasting coloured felt, cut another smaller appliqué piece, such as a bow, tulip, star, bunny or strawberry (on page 233).

3. Using small running stitches and embroidery thread in matching or contrasting shades, stitch the smaller shape into place on one of the cosy shapes for each pair.

4. Work extra details, if you like, in contrasting thread.

5. Place the two cosy shapes together, wrong sides facing each other, with the ends of your ribbon loop sandwiched between the two at the top. Using a contrasting embroidery thread, sew around the curved edge with a small running stitch.

6. Work another line of running stitch along the bottom edge of your cosy at the front, taking care not to stitch through both layers of the opening.

7. Pop your egg in its cup and dress in its charming new outfit.

Very cute vessels

After years of amassing an impressive haul of random bits and pieces for the kitchen, I recently had a big clear-out and decided to get rid of the things we're not using. I usually purge any clothes we're not wearing every six months – sometimes even more often than that – but I've found it easier to let the kitchen build up with an extraordinary amount of unused items. I think it might have something to do with our obsession with kitchenware shops and all the new gadgets on offer.

I don't like to let useless appliances and equipment take up valuable space in our kitchen, so it's great to have a spring clean every once in a while. Just as when you clear out the closets, you'll find it's actually easier to locate things with a carefully edited collection of items, and clever storage is key.

To achieve that saintly, cleansed feeling, ask everyone to chip in and help get rid of all the dust-collectors: the pasta makers, chipped ramekins you wouldn't serve anything in and the make-your-own-bread machine you used once. And try to buy only new things you know you'll use. Don't get hooked on the idea that you have to have everything tucked away in shiny new cupboards, either – if you and smaller members of the family love it or use it frequently, display it on an open shelf or rack. I like the idea of turning regular ideas about storage on their head. The Europeans are so much better at this – think of all those gorgeous Provençal and Tuscan kitchens, and the English and their Agas; those are real family homes, brimming with love! Here in Australia, we tend to renovate the life out of our kitchens until they have no atmosphere whatsoever. Down with white boxes, I say. Make a bread board from a piece of wood worn smooth by many hands, and use antique postman's pigeonholes to display favourite pieces if you like. Or keep some of the kids' favourite things in easily accessible baskets or buckets.

Following are a couple of items I've made that we find really useful – I hope you do too.

Clever bag dispenser

I'm so against plastic bags – I can't tell you how much I detest them. And the ridiculous amount of packaging on everything drives me completely crazy. So much so that I refuse to buy certain brands where the makers seem to revel in wrapping things excessively. Bore the kids and everyone in your family to death by nagging them to stop using plastic – food wrap included (a nifty selection of containers is just as good, and lasts much longer).

Sometimes, however, using plastic bags is just unavoidable, even when you carry a couple of calico or string bags in the bottom of your handbag each day. Most of the bins in our house fit recycled plastic bags, so we do have a bag to store bags in the kitchen. It couldn't be simpler to make, so ask the younger members of the household to help you construct one.

Hang this handy utilitarian item on the inside door of your pantry or in a cupboard, or go ahead and display it proudly in the kitchen. The prettier the fabric you use, the more you'll want it hanging around.

You will need

- ✳ 40 × 50 cm (16 × 20 in) cotton or canvas
- ✳ Approximately 1.1 m × 6 mm-wide (1¼ yd × ¼ in) ribbon, for the drawstrings
- ✳ Approximately 20 cm × 20 mm-wide (8 × ¾ in) woven cotton tape or ribbon, for the loop
- ✳ Safety pin
- ✳ Scissors
- ✳ Sewing machine and thread

Instructions

1. Press under 6 mm (¼ in) on the two long (50 cm/20 in) raw edges of your cotton rectangle, then press under another 6 mm and stitch this double hem in place.

2. Now fold the rectangle in half lengthwise, right sides together, aligning the hemmed edges. Beginning and ending 4 cm (1½ in) from the top and bottom raw edges, stitch the sides together to create a tube, stitching just inside the hemmed edge.

3. To create the casings, press under 6 mm (¼ in) on the top and bottom raw edges, then press under another 2 cm (¾ in) and topstitch in place close to the inner pressed edge.

4. Fold the wider length of ribbon or tape into a loop and stitch the raw ends to the inside of the bag at the top end of the seam, just below the casing. Turn the bag right side out.

5. Cut the narrow ribbon into two equal pieces and, using your safety pin, thread a piece through the casing at each end of the bag. Draw up the ribbon at each end, leaving the top end almost open for inserting bags and a hole at the bottom just wide enough to pull your bags through. Tie the ends in a bow and trim the ends diagonally to prevent fraying.

6. Fill your bag with recycled plastic bags and hang in a useful spot. *Parfait!* You're done.

Keeping little hands busy

If your young helper isn't old enough to sew one of these unassisted, ask him or her to roll all the plastic bags into little balls and then insert them into the finished dispenser. They might also like to cut simple felt shapes that could be stitched to the outside of the bag for extra decoration.

Papier mâché fruit bowl

Now, here is one of the very best projects in this book to make with children, because *anyone* can make papier mâché. There are no rules for keeping it clean, and budding abstract artists will relish the opportunity to slop glue, paper and paint around and still create something quite impressive. But you might want to make sure they're wearing a painting smock first (see page 131 for instructions on how to construct one).

Make no mistake: this is going to be messy!

*Tip

If you're a little too impatient to wait days for your papier mâché to dry, you can always pop it in the oven. Make sure you leave the oven door propped open while your bowl is drying, and that you keep a constant eye on the piece as it dries so that it doesn't get too hot and become a fire risk.

You will need

* Chicken wire in a small cross-hatch, usually available from a hardware store or garden nursery

* Tin snips

* Newspaper

* Wallpaper adhesive (available from paint and hardware stores) and water

* Oven

* Acrylic paint

* Paintbrush

Instructions

1. Mix up your wallpaper adhesive as per the instructions on the back of the pack. You will need to leave it sitting for a bit to coagulate, so make sure you make the glue first.

2. Use your tin snips to cut a circle, roughly 40 cm (16 in) in diameter from your roll of chicken wire. This step should be done by an adult – the jaws of tin snips are fierce enough to cut off a finger or two!

3. Fold the sharp edges of the wire over on themselves, then start to fashion the circle into a bowl shape by bending the sides up and around, folding excess wire flat against itself. This will be the base of your bowl and, once the basic bending and folding is completed, it's now a good time to hand it over to your helper to finish off.

4. Lay out a few sheets of newspaper on your work space or table to protect it from drips.

5. Rip another few sheets of newspaper into 3–4 cm-wide (1$\frac{1}{4}$–1$\frac{1}{2}$-in) strips.

6. Dip a strip into the adhesive mixture before pinching the end of the strip and running your fingers along it to remove as much excess glue as possible.

7. Wrap the strip around your chicken wire frame, starting at the sharp edges around the rim of the bowl.

8. Continue using your strips to cover the entire frame, overlapping at the edges.

9. When the bowl is finished, you need to let it get completely dry and hard. The traditional – and best – way to do this is to leave it somewhere warm and dry for a few weeks until it is ready. You can, however, if you're impatient like me, hurry things along by using the oven, but remember that your bowl is more likely to warp and you may not get it completely dry in the centre, which can lead to mould growing. Turn your oven on to about 180°C (350°F), and leave the door open. Pop the bowl, upside down, on one of the wire racks in the oven to dry – depending on how much adhesive you've used, it should take between 30 and 90 minutes.

10. When your bowl is dry, paint it with a few coats of bright acrylic paint and leave to dry overnight. Decorate with some delicious-looking fruit and pop it, pride of place, on the kitchen table.

Dress-ups

I am (at least mildly) obsessed with dressing up. Before I even found out what flavour we were having, I'd collected a wonderful old antique chest and the first items to make a dress-ups box for our new arrival. Ever practical, I left the purchasing of useful things like a cot, a pram and newborn clothes to the very end (and mainly to her proud papa) while I set Olive's priorities straight in utero. I'm probably lining myself up for disappointment (yes, I will be devastated if she has no interest whatsoever in clothes), but I'm sure I'll cope somehow.

The dress-ups box is not just about pretty, flouncy frocks. Nor is it strictly secret girls' business either, oh no! Masks, wigs, crazy clompy shoes, gloves, stage makeup and hats all play a vital role in creating new identities in this very best of playtime activities. The dress-ups box – which I can remember messing about in from as early as three – formed the very basis of my identity. Indeed, I don't know where I'd be without it. In a far less fun place, I suspect.

Masquerade provides a wonderful basis for encouraging imagination in kids. What child wouldn't enjoy exploring the possibility of life as a pirate, or a queen, or a crafty Puss-in-boots? Give them the tools to inspire these fancies and leave them to get on with it (perhaps sneaking in now and then to admire how delicious they look... they're only so little and unselfconscious for so long, after all).

I confess that I get a great deal of pleasure from dressing our girl each day. Who doesn't experience a thrill making their loved ones look good? I have tried very hard to avoid the mini-me situation, but I'm afraid there are still days when we leave the house without realising I've popped her in something very similar, or at least matching in colour, because I'm obviously in the mood for red or blue or whatever I've chosen. It takes a conscious effort to do otherwise.

I'm sure Olive will have something to say about this when she develops a will of her own (and, given her parents, I'm fairly certain it's going to be a strong one) but for now, I will continue to make her the following things and enjoy dressing her up in them. If you're already dealing with a fussy child, involve them in the colour, fabric and decoration choices before you get chopping and sewing. That way, hopefully, your work won't be in vain and they will always wear their kid-friendly couture with pride.

Cute-as-pie clothing

I have to admit that this chapter is the main reason I wanted to write *The Crafty Kid*. While making things for my last book, I got so ridiculously *into* playing with felt (the Lichtenstein-inspired felt fridge magnets 'Bang' and 'Pow' are, without a doubt, my favourite things in *The Crafty Minx*… maybe they were also a little inspired by the fact I was watching the excellent Western, *3:10 to Yuma*, while creating them) that I started dreaming of other felt fancies. That's when I warmed to the idea of writing a book of things to make exclusively for and with children – particularly items they could wear.

I have also been going to some amazing design fairs and children's shops since then, where I've seen the most achingly beautiful clothes in miniature… I want them for myself. But the ideas behind them are so simple, really. Recently, I went nuts buying Olive some plain footless tights, striped tops, frocks, stretchy skirts and divine tutus, and set about decorating them myself. And I found a pair of brown Blundstone boots at the markets to go with the clothes: they look ace.

If you can make or adorn a few simple items of clothing for children, you'll be able to re-create some of the most stylish kids' fashions around and save yourself a load of dosh in the process, because these *Studio Bambini*-style looks come at a steep price in the chicest children's wear stores. Adorn affordable basics from Bonds or Target with your unique creations, pair with the higher-end children's fashion and – just as with adults' clothes – you'll be able to construct a wearable, stylish wardrobe for your little ones to see them through their formative years.

The key things to always look out for are stretchy separates – such as tops, tights and gorgeous knits with a bit of give in them – as well as good, hardy tunics and smocks. They're great for layering and can last for years. Buy the big-ticket items less often – this will be very important as they grow. And don't forget about natural fibres and good quality, overall. You'll thank me when that jumper is still looking fresh (rather than nasty and ball-y) after countless washes.

Handsome appliquéd pirate shirt

I'm sorry about the bias towards making things for little girls in this book: this is my attempt to redress the balance. I'm sure if I had a boy, I'd do a better job at coming up with ideas for boyish things to make but hopefully, you'll be able to think of ways to adapt some of these projects if you do have a wee man in your life instead.

Here's an idea for a boy's present, but there's no reason why you can't make one for a favourite girl if you so choose. A jaunty skull and crossbones is perfectly acceptable attire for both sexes, if you ask me, but not everyone will agree. Given the right red skirt, I'd even wear one. *High seas, here we come!*

✳Tip

This appliqué pattern for a skull and crossbones also looks great on a square blue cushion. Copy the same instructions but apply to a cushion cover rather than a top and ta-daa: you have yourself a pirate pillow. Feel free to replace the black denim with white calico if you prefer your bones sun-bleached.

Ahoy, me hearties!

You will need

* Small pieces of colourfast black fabric or denim (as I've used here)
* Red fabric (patterned or not) for the bandanna
* Blue-and-white striped long-sleeved top, or any other plain top
* Scissors
* Bobble-headed pins
* Sewing machine and black thread

Instructions

1. Using the pattern outlines on page 241, cut out the skull and crossbones shapes from your black denim and the bandanna from red cotton.

2. Lay out your shapes on the front of the striped top and pin into place.

3. Set your machine to a zigzag stitch and, ruching up the back of the top to keep it out of the way, sew around the edges to secure the appliqué in place to the front while removing the pins. Be careful not to stitch through both layers of fabric... and that's all there is to it.

Tea party felt

Nothing beats a good tea party, folks.

Back around the time of the handover back to the Chinese, I was living and working in Hong Kong, where one of my favourite pastimes was going to a traditional tea house with friends. Forget the bars – High Tea is where it's at! On a trip to Shanghai once, my first stop was, quite literally, the old Peace Hotel (the epicentre of opium trading back in the Jazz Age) to soak up the atmosphere of the former ballroom – the epicentre of the epicentre – over tea and petits fours. I left my luggage with the concierge and waltzed right on in. And the best hen-do I ever went to (oh alright, I organised it) started with High Tea and champagne. I mean it: nothing beats a good tea party. You get dressed up, treat yourself with miniature, sinful sweets, and drink lots and lots of tea. What's not to love?

When Olive was but two months old, I bought her her first tea set. Pink with white spots and teeny, tiny cups, we've already tried sharing a strawberries-and-cream-flavoured fruit tisane. Olive gave me a funny look when I tried to help her drink it but no matter; she has time to develop a full-blown tea addiction like mine.

Here is another idea for adorning children's clothes. This appliquéd scene looks adorable placed like this or making its way around the bottom hem of a frock or skirt, but is equally fetching across the front of a top or stitched to the lapels of a cardigan. The trick is to play around with your pieces first, working out the spot which suits them best before sewing into place. A few inches up, down, left or right can make all the difference, but feel free to copy their placement here if you don't feel confident messing around with your own version. I've added a row of pompoms along the bottom of this simple white frock to pick up the colour from the pot and saucer, which I think is super-cute.

You will need

✳ Felt in red, yellow and blue, plus pink and cream for the tea and cup's insides, as I've used

✳ Scissors

✳ Matching/contrasting embroidery thread and sewing needle

✳ A favourite item of clothing

Instructions

1. Cut out the shapes on pattern page 235.

2. Place the spots on top of the tea pot and stitch into place.

3. Lay the cup over the saucer and stitch into place.

4. Stitch around the rim of teacup and teapot.

5. Now play around with the placement and stitch to your favourite item of clothing.

Keeping little hands busy

Depending on how deft your little one is with scissors, help them to cut the felt shapes, or present them with their own set of pre-cut shapes and encourage them to arrange the spots on the pot, the cup on the saucer and so on.

You could also cut out a little cake and let them add the icing and cherry on top!

Renovated skirt

More often than not, the clothes I buy for myself have been pre-loved, so I'm used to making a few minor alterations here and there: some new buttons, a lower neckline, or shortening sleeves and hems to suit. If I'm feeling adventurous, I'll pop in a new panel or create pockets and other useful features. But still, I don't have the confidence (actually, the patience) to make all but the most simple clothes from scratch.

Softies and mobiles and blankets are so satisfying to make because they're quick and easy, and are also very forgiving if you make a mistake (just pretend you *meant* for the legs of your sock monkey to be different lengths). And alterations are great because you can totally reinvent something without reinventing the wheel. But the thought of following one of the many Vogue patterns I have been buying rather ambitiously for years sets my teeth on edge.

In that spirit, I've been making lots of little-girl skirts lately out of full-sized ladies' skirts. I first had the idea when I found this beauty on the next page, from Liberty of London, at a market stall for £2. It was ridiculously teensy for a grown woman (I could barely get it over my thighs) and refused to zip up at the back, but I had to have it for the fabric alone. Initially, I chopped some off to make a D-ring belt, and a panel for a friend's doorstop as a thank you for inviting us to supper. Then I realised that if I just brought in the sides, it would make a gorgeous skirt for a young girl.

Buy ladies' skirts – the smaller the better, because tiny sizes always languish, waiting to be bought in charity stores for much longer – and give them a new lease of life. 1960s and '70s-era designs serve well, because floral, spriggy numbers were very 'in' back then, and these (along with some of the peasant styles from that era, with hand-embroidering or beading) look divine on little girls.

You will need

* One ladies' skirt
* Measuring tape
* Dressmaker's chalk
* Scissors
* Sewing machine and thread
* Optional: elastic, about 1 cm (^{3}/$_8$ in) wide and long enough to fit around your girl's waist

Instructions

1. Measure the circumference of your little girl's waist with a tape measure, and her height from waist to knee.

2. Wrap the tape measure around the waistband of the skirt, and work out how much it will need to be brought in at either side to fit – make sure you add an extra 4 cm (1^1/$_2$ in) in total for the 1 cm (^{3}/$_8$ in) seam allowance on each panel, and make a mark with your chalk. You might also want to cut fabric from just the one side, particularly if it has a zip on the other side which you can still use.

3. Measure the height from waist to knee-length and make a mark here also, adding an extra 2 cm (^{3}/$_4$ in) for the hem. If you plan to use elastic at the waist, remember to allow for a casing (see page 74).

4. Use your scissors to chop off any excess fabric from the sides and bottom hem.

5. With the right sides together, sew the sides to each other with your machine, and add an extra line of zigzag stitching to stop it fraying.

6. Turn up your bottom hem, tuck the raw edge under and topstitch the hem in place. Thread elastic through casing, if using. Yes, it really is that simple.

Keeping little hands busy

Why not take your little one along with you on a shopping trip to choose their favourite skirts from a charity store? It's never too soon, I say!

Some more tips for renovating skirts

✳ To make a skirt last even longer, pop in an elasticated waistband – this works well if the original skirt doesn't have a zip or if you decide to cut it off from the sides. Simply fold over the casing on the waist edge, leaving enough width to thread through your elastic, and sew in place (leaving the ends of the tube open). Attach a safety pin to your elastic and work through one end of the tube until you reach the end, before sewing in place at the seams.

✳ You might also want to fold the fabric up at the hem rather than cut it; this way, it can be taken down as little girls become not-so-little.

✳ Another idea for skirts that become too short but not too tight around the waist is to sew on an additional piece of fabric to create a false hem. Try using a beautiful strip of broderie anglaise, or the lacy edge from a pre-loved antique tablecloth.

✳ This isn't going to make your skirt any longer, but think about adding a row of pompoms or tasselled fringing to the bottom of your skirt. It looks super-cute and will totally transform the hem of a plain skirt or frock.

'Sweet dreams' nightdress

Make this sweet nightdress for a wee girl from a recycled pillowcase, ribbon and some rickrack. Depending on the fabric you use, it can also be worn as a summer frock, or as a tunic over a cotton tee or skivvy.

This pillowcase, one of a pair, was a great find. Judging from its loud and acid-bright design, I think it's from the 1960s or '70s and cost all of 50 cents at our local charity store. Add the cost of a few metres of lavish rickrack and ribbon, and it was still less than $10 to make. And the very best thing? I've tried this on both a girl of three and a girl of eight, and it fitted both of them beautifully – it was just longer on the three-year-old. Smock styles look great on most girls and will last almost forever in their wardrobes.

*Tip

If your pillowcase is too wide for your little girl, you can always take it in a bit at the sides, but use a longer stitch and keep the extra few inches of fabric inside so you can unpick when they get bigger.

You will need

* Standard pillowcase
* About 1.8 m (2 yd) rickrack
* About 1.3 m × 20 mm-wide (1³/8 yd × ³/4 in) ribbon
* Scissors
* Sewing machine and thread
* Safety pin

Instructions

1. Lay out your pillowcase on a table, and cut across the bottom (closed) edge, so the pillowcase is now a tube that is open at both ends.

2. Press under 6 mm (¹/4 in) on the raw edge you have just cut, then press under another 3 cm (1¹/4 in) and topstitch the hem in place.

3. Stitch a length of rickrack over the stitching line on the hem edge.

4. At the top opening of the tube, cut a slightly tapered armhole into the fabric on one side, then repeat for the other side, taking care that the armholes match.

5. The top front edge of the pillowcase should already have a 2.5 cm-wide (1 in) hem – wide enough for a casing to fit your ribbon through. Unpick the hemmed edges by about 5 cm (2 in) on each side.

6. The folded edge of the pillowcase will now be opened up, so cut off any excess fabric, leaving enough to create a double hem to match the front edge, but do not sew it in place yet.

7. Roll under a very narrow double hem on the raw edges of the armholes and stitch in place.

8. Now re-stitch the hemmed edge on the top front, and re-fold and stitch the double hem on the top back, thus creating a neat casing on both top edges for your ribbon.

9. Stitch a length of rickrack over the casing seam on both front and back, folding the rickrack ends under at the sides of the dress and sewing flat.

10. Attach your safety pin to one end of your length of ribbon, then thread through casing at the front of the dress, then across the shoulder and through the back casing as well.

11. When you get back to the starting point, pull up the ribbon so the neck edge of the dress is gathered and tie the ribbon in a bow at one shoulder. Neaten ribbon ends diagonally to prevent fraying.

Mini A-line dress or tunic

This is one item of clothing anyone can be brave enough to attempt making from scratch. My favourite things about A-line dresses are: they need a very minimal amount of fitting to look good, and can be worn on their own or with a bright top underneath, depending on the season. There's also really no age or era when an A-line doesn't look chic (says she, the perennial A-line fan.)

You can construct an A-line dress out of virtually any fabric (remember when Maria chopped up the Von Trapp family curtains in *The Sound of Music*? Sometimes it takes a bit of wartime deprivation to get people thinking creatively) but 100% cotton denim and corduroy are cheap, cheerful and work so well for this item of clothing, which doubles as a good winter tunic. And the denim makes it nice and sturdy for hyperactive mesdemoiselles.

*Tip

If you're nervous, as I am, about using the buttonhole function on your sewing machine, simply lap the back shoulder straps over the front and sew the buttons into place through all layers. You can then simply snip the buttons off and move them further up the straps as she grows bigger; providing her head fits through the neck-hole.

You will need

✳ Dark blue denim

✳ Red cotton corduroy

✳ Cute design for appliqué patch

✳ Measuring tape

✳ Dressmaker's chalk

✳ Scissors

✳ Sewing machine and thread

✳ Two big buttons

✳ Needle and thread

Instructions

1. Firstly, use your tape measure and a pencil to make a note of your little girl's width across the widest part of her chest from one armpit to the other. Add an extra 4 cm (1^{1}/$_{2}$ in) to this measurement, for ease. Now measure her height, from shoulder to knee (or where your want the dress to come to).

2. Lay out your denim on the table, wrong side facing up, and chalk out the measurements into a basic rectangle. Rule a line down the centre of the rectangle, from top to bottom.

3. Enlarge the pattern piece for the Front (on page 232), until the width of the chest measurement just fits in one half of your rectangle. The A-line edge of the pattern piece will extend beyond the edge of your ruled rectangle. Trace around the pattern piece, then flip it over, along the centre front line, and trace the other side, giving you one complete Front.

4. Now add 1 cm (^{3}/$_{8}$ in) seam allowance around the sides and upper edges, plus 4 cm (1^{1}/$_{2}$ in) on the lower edge.

5. Repeat Steps 2–4, this time using the pattern piece for the Back.

6. Cut out both Front and Back pieces on your outer traced lines.

7. For the Front and Back Facings, cut your pattern pieces along the facing line shown on the pattern and use them to cut one complete Front Facing and one complete Back Facing, from corduroy.

8. Cut a small pocket shape from a scrap of leftover corduroy.

9. Sew your appliqué patch to the front of the dress, using a zigzag stitch to prevent fraying.

10. Turn under a narrow double hem on the top edge of the pocket and topstitch in place.

11. Now press under 6 mm (^{1}/$_{4}$ in) on the remaining raw edges of the pocket. Position the pocket on the front left-hand side of the dress and topstitch into place close to the pressed edges.

12. With right sides together and allowing 1 cm (³/8 in) seams, stitch the front of the dress to the back of the dress at the side seams. Press seams open.

13. With right sides together and allowing 1 cm (³/8 in) seams, stitch the front facing to the back facing at both the side seams. Press seams open.

14. To prevent fraying, finish the lower straight edge of the facing with a narrow double hem or zigzag.

15. Now, with right sides together, raw edges even, and matching side seams, pin the facing to the dress around the front, back and armhole edges. Allowing a 1 cm (³/8 in) seam, stitch as pinned, removing the pins as you go.

16. Clip across the seam allowance close to the stitching on the curves, then turn the facing to the inside and press well.

17. Starting at one underarm seam, topstitch right around the finished neck and armhole edges of the dress, stitching about 6 mm (¹/4 in) from the edge.

18. Press up and stitch a narrow double hem on the lower edge of the dress.

19. Sew a buttonhole into each end of the back shoulder straps and, on the front shoulder straps, sew on buttons to correspond.

20. Shimmy over your girl's head and button up.

Keeping little hands busy

Ask your A-line recipient to choose her favourite fabric for the front panel, and some matching (or mismatching) buttons for decoration. She could even help sew on the front panel with a running stitch herself.

Cold weather cosies

This chapter is all about gorgeous knits – and you don't even have to pick up a pair of knitting needles to make them.

The amount of inventive things to do with old jumpers is staggering, and yet so many people chuck them out once they're sporting a few holes or stains. I know this, because my local charity store and flea market have a never-ending supply of pre-loved woolly bits and pieces, and I'm constantly snapping them up for a few dollars each. I hate to think how many simply end up in the bin, creating yet more landfill.

There are loads of items that don't even have a thing wrong with them, and many have never been worn – these I put aside for myself, James, Olive and friends I know would appreciate them. I've found so many small, lovingly hand-knitted pieces for Olive at the markets, that I've actually had to stop buying them for a while. My favourite is a gorgeous, powder-blue lambswool cardigan, which I can just imagine someone's grandmother spending an age knitting for a beloved child. It looks like it may have been worn once or twice, if at all, and I'm thrilled we've been able to extend its life for a few years yet.

Sometimes, the pieces I find are fine to wear as is after a gentle wash, and sometimes I pop on a covered button or two, or appliqué some pretty fabric to the lapels or hem. It's amazing how expensive this treatment can make an old jumper look. I don't like fussy adornment myself, but if you can master the art of minimally decorating plain pieces, you'll not only be able to create a beautiful wardrobe for your family on a budget, but your clothes will be truly unique. And I'd bet money on the fact that you end up loving them more than chain-store pieces as well, after a bit of judicious trimming with some lovely buttons, say, or a cute iron-on patch.

Oddly shaped, holey or stained pieces can be chopped up for a whole range of things. I do turn my nose up at acrylic because it just wears so badly and doesn't usually feel very nice against the skin. Look at the labels for the pure wool mark – I think lambswool and cashmere, in particular, are the best to go for. I'm not a huge fan of alpaca or mohair because they can be quite scratchy, and some people are allergic to rabbit angora. Rub jumpers between your fingers – sometimes a very small amount (5–10%) of nylon is virtually undetectable, and can be fine for certain projects. And be aware that hand-knitted pieces unravel much more easily once they've been cut – you'll need to stitch them together more firmly than machine knits.

It often amazes me when covetable designer pieces are made from man-made fibres. It seems such a cheat, especially when you're paying a hefty premium for the label in the first place. Sadly, I do see piles and piles of clothes at charity stores that aren't worth bothering to recycle, and they always seem to be made from nasty acrylics. But the biggest offenders at making throwaway fashion are usually the high-street chain stores, which is why I boycott buying these types of clothes.

Look out for gorgeous second-hand fabrics – particularly wool – and start recycling them for your craft projects. Even the smallest pieces can be useful for appliqué or, if in a sorry state, to stuff inside a soft toy (just chop them up into tiny pieces first to stop it being lumpy). And don't throw something away if it's comfy and you still enjoy wearing it around the house. I've always thought there's something rather chic about slightly dishevelled homewear anyway – well-worn jeans and voluminous boyfriend jumpers, for example. What nicer way to end the day than to come home, slip off the work-day clothes and cuddle up in your roomiest, softest pieces? When you have children, this is the only way to save yourself several loads of washing each week, as your (and their) best clothes will be tucked away safely from all the mess that comes with a lovely home life.

Two brilliant neck-warmers

Sometimes a cold or flu can drag on forever, no matter how many early nights and vitamins we stock up on. The icy weather doesn't help, and often the only way to be comfortable outside in the elements is with a soft woolly scarf wrapped, many times, around the neck and chest area to keep out the chill.

I do so love to see little ones rugged up in their winter woollies, and get such a kick out of dressing Olive in deliciously soft knits so that only her rosy cheeks and little face are exposed to the winter winds (flu or no flu). Here are two very simple ideas for rugging up wee necks with cleverly refashioned materials – you won't be able to throw a t-shirt or polo-necked jumper out in future without making one of these, now you know how easily it's done.

T-shirt scarf

Made from cotton jersey or an old t-shirt destined for the rag bag, here's a scarf that can be worn in any weather and looks cute either knotted about the neck or casually flung over a shoulder, Isadora Duncan-style (and sensibly worn a little less trailing!).

You will need

✳ Cotton jersey material or one old t-shirt

✳ Scissors

✳ Small scrap of fabric in a pretty design for appliqué patch

✳ Bobble-headed pins

✳ Embroidery needle and thread

Instructions

1. Recycle an old t-shirt by cutting a strip, from the bottom hem at the front, up over the shoulder seam and down to the bottom hem at the back – this should give you a scarf about 10–15 cm (4–6 in) wide and at least 80 cm (31 in) long. And the best thing: t-shirt jersey doesn't really fray, so you don't need to hem the edges.

2. If the t-shirt has a seam at the shoulder you will have a line of stitching across the middle of the scarf. Use your needle and thread to reinforce this seam with a couple of stitches at each end to prevent it from unravelling.

3. If you're using jersey fabric, rather than a t-shirt, cut a strip of about 25 cm (10 in) wide × the width of the fabric and cut off the selvedges so the edges will curl nicely.

4. Take your pins and fix your scrap of prettily-patterned fabric to the front of the scarf at one end.

5. Hand-stitch with embroidery thread around the outside with small, firm, overcasting stitches.

6. Tie around a small neck in a nonchalant fashion, showing off the featured appliqué patch.

Pretty polo-necked scarves

Ask a lazy person to perform a job and they'll discover the easiest way to do it. That's how I came up with the idea for these. Much easier than knitting them yourself!

There's no need for instructions – simply cut the neck off any old, soft polo-necked jumper at the spot where the seams join, as I've done with a beautiful blue cashmere number and some red lambswool seen on the previous page. If it's too wide for your little one's neck, you can take it in a bit at one side (but it should still be wide enough to stretch over their head). Sew on a pretty covered button or two for decoration and *voilà*, you're done.

Keeping little hands busy

There's no reason why children can't make these all on their own, as long as they can be trusted with scissors. A few stitches are all that's needed to secure buttons in place as well, although you might want to check their stitches are firm enough.

Soft-soled socks

I love padding about the house in socks rather than shoes, especially when it's cold and especially because our home is laid with floorboards rather than carpet – I just have to be careful not to slip. That's why these soft-soled socks are excellent for roaming about the house in: the sole means you'll have better grip, and traction's always good for giddy little ones when they're moving too quickly. But make sure they stay inside: attempting to walk about on concrete and other outdoor surfaces will quickly reduce them to shreds!

Depending on the leather you use, these socks should even be soft enough to hop into bed with (just give them a bit of a brush by hand first to avoid bringing floor grit in with you). Perfect for sleepy little ones, who want to simply crawl into dreams after an exhausting day of play.

You will need

* An old jumper – a smaller ladies' jumper or one that has been shrunk a little by accident in the wash will work better for creating socks for children, as you'll be wasting less fabric

* Small patches of very soft or pliable leather or suede for the soles (I found my mismatched pieces at Reverse Garbage, a recycling depot near my home)

* Measuring tape (optional)

* Scissors

* Bobble-headed pins

* Sewing machine and thread

* Leather needle

Instructions

1. Lay out your jumper on a table.

2. Measure the length of your child's leg and foot, from mid-calf to big toe, or simply hold one sleeve of your jumper against the child's leg and foot, with the cuff at the calf.

3. Make a mark where the toes end, adding a little extra for wriggle-room and seam allowance.

4. Use your scissors to chop across both jumper sleeves at the same spot, rounding the edges in a curve for the toes. If your jumper is small, you may be able to use the actual tube of the sleeve as it is and simply sew across the toe end; if it is too wide for your child's leg, you will need to take it in by adding a side seam from the toe up to the cuff.

5. Now take your leather and cut out a shape to roughly match the sole of your little one's foot (ask him or her to stand on some newspaper and draw around the foot if you're unsure) then pin the leather shapes to the outside of the sole area of the sock.

6. Set your machine to a small zigzag stitch and stitch the leather to your sock around the edges, reversing a few times at the end for strength. If your sock is a tube shape, take care that you are only stitching through one layer.

7. Turn the sock inside out and then sew up the open edges around the toe end and up the side, if you are making it narrower.

8. Turn socks right side out again and slip on your child's feet so they're all warm and toasty.

Keeping little hands busy

While you're chopping up a jumper, cut a couple of extra squares and help your child thread a blunt-ended tapestry needle with wool yarn. Show them how to do a simple running stitch around the edges.

This can then be turned into a little cushion, a simple bag or even a woolly hat for a favourite soft toy.

Envelope finger mittens

Remember those frosty mornings in winter on the way to school? When your breath created a plume of steam in the air and every exposed centimetre of skin begged to be hidden under cosy wool? I do – protect your little ones from the same fate.

These are mittens of the most useful variety: rather than taking them off when hunting around in your wallet for spare change, or when kiddies want to investigate an interesting flower or toy further, simply flip the top over the fingers so they are free to be more dexterous.

When you're done making them, attach woolly plaits to the wrists to keep pairs from disappearing off on their own solo travels. They're so lovely and comfortable, they'll never want to take them off.

You will need

∗ Scrap paper or cardboard and a pencil

∗ An old jumper – a smaller ladies' jumper or one that has been shrunk a little by accident in the wash will work better for creating mittens for children, as you'll be wasting less fabric

∗ Dressmaker's chalk

∗ Scissors

∗ Measuring tape

∗ Embroidery needle and thread for embellishments (optional)

∗ Needle and cotton thread

∗ Ball of fine wool (to use as thread)

∗ Tapestry needle

Instructions

1. Lay your piece of paper on a flat surface. Place your child's hand on the paper, asking them to keep all their fingers together with the thumb splayed out slightly. Trace around the hand shape with your pencil, adding about 4–5 cm (1^1/$_2$–2 in) below the wrist bone for the cuff.

2. Send them off to play again and add about 3 cm (1^1/$_4$ in) around the curved edges of your traced line (not the cuff edge): 1 cm (^{3}/$_8$ in) for the seam allowance and the rest for wiggle room. Cut out on your traced line. This is your mitten pattern.

3. Lay one sleeve of your jumper out flat and place your mitten pattern on top, aligning the straight cuff edge of the pattern with the finished cuff of the sleeve.

4. Trace around the outline with chalk, then use your scissors to cut out the mitten shape along the traced line, through both layers of the sleeve. These two shapes will make the mitten tops for each hand.

5. If you want to add any embellishment to your mittens, such as a little chain-stitched heart, it's easier to do this now, before the mittens are constructed. When you're finished, set the tops aside for the moment.

6. Now, measure down about 9 cm (3^1/$_2$ in) from the top edge of your paper mitten pattern and rule a line across the pattern at this point. Cut your pattern in two across the ruled line and save both pieces.

7. Take the other sleeve and, starting at the cuff edge, align the lower part of your mitten pattern to the cuff of the sleeve (as for the mitten top). Trace around the pattern with chalk, but add an extra 2.5 cm (1 in) above the straight edge. Cut out, through both layers.

8. Now put the remaining upper section of the pattern on the sleeve and trace around the pattern with chalk, but add an extra 2.5 cm (1 in) below the straight edge. Cut out, through both layers.

9. Turn under 6 mm (^{1}/$_4$ in) on the straight edge of each half-mitten section and stitch in place by hand, using a needle and thread and small stitches.

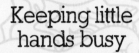

Keeping little hands busy

Ask your child to make the plaits that keep these mittens together. They could also cut simple, favourite shapes from felt which could be appliquéd to the tops of each one.

10. With the right sides facing up, lap the hemmed edge of an upper mitten section over the corresponding hemmed edge of a lower mitten section until the mitten shape is exactly the same size as the mitten top. Catch in place with a couple of stitches at each side, to keep the lapped edges in place. Repeat this step for the remaining two half-mitten sections. You now have two mitten bottoms, with a clever lapped opening in the centre.

11. Place the mittens together in pairs (a top and a bottom) with their right sides facing each other.

12. Using your tapestry needle and matching wool thread, backstitch around the outer edges of the mittens, popping in a few extra stitches at the lapped edges for extra strength. Turn the mittens right side out.

13. Measure and cut six 25 cm (10 in) lengths of wool.

14. Make two simple plaits of three lengths each, tying knots in either end.

15. Attach one end of a plait to the inside wrist of each mitten with a few small stitches.

16. Tie the mittens together with a bow and sling over a hook for later use, or tuck the plaits inside and pop on your little one's hands straight away, before sending them out into the frosty winter air.

Decorated cardigan

As I've mentioned, our local charity store is a brilliant source of hand-knitted pieces for children – I've found three divine pure wool cardigans there, which had never been worn (including this one), and each cost less than a takeaway coffee. Red, blue and yellow, they are all made of the finest lambswool and must have taken ages to knit. Cardigans are a great wardrobe staple and because they can be worn open, they look great either outsized, about the right fit, or looking shrunken just to keep the arms warm over a short-sleeved frock.

I prefer simple designs (no hippie rainbows for us) but a little decoration goes a long way to making a plain cardigan look quite special, and far more upmarket than it actually is. The same principle also applies to a cardigan for a grown woman.

*Tip

It is best to cut your fabric strip on the bias (that is, at 45 degrees to the straight grain) because bias fabric has some stretch and it will sit more neatly around the curve of the neckline.

You will need

✳ A knitted cardigan

✳ A bias strip of cotton in a contrasting design, about 3 cm (1¼ in) wide and long enough to cover both open sides and the neck area (see Tip)

✳ Sewing needle and thread

✳ Covered button

Instructions

1. Starting at the bottom of one opening edge of your cardigan and leaving a little overlap, lay the cotton strip along the edge of the knit, right sides together and edges matching. Using a needle and thread (or the sewing machine, if you prefer) sew the strip into place along the edge of the cardigan, allowing a 6 mm (¼ in) seam and using small stitches.

2. Keep sewing along the front, then around the neck edge and back down the other side until you've reached the other end.

3. Fold under 6 mm (¼ in) on the remaining raw edge of the strip, then fold the pressed edge to the wrong side of the cardigan and catch in place over your previous seam with small neat stitches, turning under the raw edges at either end as well.

4. Now take your covered button and attach in a pleasing spot, somewhere near the lapel on one side at the front of the cardigan. Doesn't that look gorgeous?

Keeping little hands busy

Ask your little one to choose and sew on the button, and just keep an eye on them to make sure they don't sew front and back together.

Lovely little accoutrements

Too much glitter and glitz on young girls is not my *tasse de thé*. But that's not to say I don't adore dressing girls up and seeing them in cute things, as long as a line is not crossed. I'm afraid mini high-heels, pants with 'Princess' written across the rear end and hoop earrings (unless worn as part of a fancy dress pirate outfit, clipped on) definitely fall into the category of 'over the line' for me. And seeing young girls in make-up just makes me sad – they've got the rest of their lives to obsess over how they look; why start early? Boys in too-grown-up clothes worry me as well, frankly.

Pompom necklaces and food-themed decoration are A-OK though, in my book, because they are not too serious, and childish in a way that is appealing. To this end, the French cannot be surpassed in style when it comes to children's wear and accessories. I've spent years admiring the superb, simple beauty of their little girls' frocks, the rightness of shrunken blazers and pea-coats for boys, and just the many little decorative touches that make French children so very stylish (maybe I was Madeline in a former life?). And hurrah, now I have my own little living doll to dress.

My friend Olivier Dupon used to trade under the chic French homewares and clothing store Lola et Moi, which has since closed down. Bringing a little taste of France to inner-city Sydney, he sourced everything from ceramics, sofa cushions and jewellery to children's toys and fancy dress outfits made in small quantities by little-known French artisans. It was very inspiring, especially since (*mais, oui*) we can't all make the trip to Paris every year. The inspiration for the following things I attribute, largely, to his quirky taste and innate sense of style – and those talented artisans who have so influenced my taste over time. There's even something in here for the boys – woo hoo!

Cupcake hair clips

J'adore cupcakes. Especially the teeny, tiny kind, delicately iced, although they're so adorable-looking it can actually be hard to take that first bite and ruin them.

You can make one or a pair of these in no time at all, so they're perfect for a little girl's birthday present or just something nice to make for a favourite niece if you have a few moments to spare. Use ordinary-sized hairclips – big enough for grown-up girls to wear also – or hunt down the miniature kind for especially wee girls. You should be able to find them in most chemists or supermarkets. The cupcake design here also looks lovely on a brooch back or appliquéd to the lapel of a favourite cardigan or coat, so please don't feel restricted to using them only as hair clips.

The finished product looks good enough to eat, don't you think?

Keeping little hands busy

Who says cupcakes need to be tiny and delicately crafted? Why not let your little one attempt making one from altogether larger pieces of felt, and turn it into a cloche or school bag adornment?

You will need

* Felt in at least three (edible-looking) shades

* Small pair of scissors

* Embroidery needle and thread

* Hair clip

Instructions

1. Using the templates on page 230, first trace and cut out your base, in the rough shape of an entire cupcake. Here I've used brown felt for chocolate and cream for vanilla sponge.

2. Then cut out your icing in another shade. There's no need for it to look precise – homemade cupcakes would have the icing spilling over the sides.

3. Cut out a mini chocolate or cherry to sit on top and then secure the whole thing in place with tiny stitches.

4. Make small lines of stitching up the sides of the cupcake base to denote the paper cup it sits in.

5. Now place on the end of your hairclip and stitch to the prongs with small, firm stitches holding it in place.

Bonbon and ice-cream brooches

Okay, so one of the reasons I might think food-themed decoration is A Good Thing is because I am always thinking of the next delicious thing I'd like to cook for our next meal. It has forever been the case and thus shall it remain forever more, I suspect. And not just our next meal, but the little treat to follow it. Everything in moderation, remember? There's nothing wrong with bonbons and icecreams once in a while, if you ask me.

Yet another of my forays into felt, these ice-cream brooches are too, too simple to make and look divine on a child's lapel or breast pocket. They might also satisfy any cravings little ones have for the real thing (you wish!).

You will need

✳ Felt in pink, brown, cream and cherry red, as well as any other bright shades you fancy for the bonbons

✳ Small scissors

✳ Embroidery needle and thread

✳ Brooch backs

Instructions

1. Using the templates on page 231, trace and cut out the complete shape of the waffle cone and ice-cream on top (a simple cone shape with a rounded top) from either the brown or cream felt and then cut another one the same shape. (Two layers will make it nice and thick enough to sit stiffly as a brooch.)

2. Now cut out your strawberry ice-cream from the pink felt, or chocolate or vanilla, as long as the flavour contrasts with the cone (otherwise you'll end up with a very boring-looking, not to mention boring-tasting, ice-cream).

3. Cut out a cherry and a chocolate or vanilla wafer to stick on top of the ice-cream.

4. Now, using your embroidery needle and thread, sew the whole concoction together, sewing the two cones together first, then adding the ice-cream and finally the toppings.

5. For the bonbons, cut two Bonbon shapes from contrasting colours, one slightly larger than the other, as shown. Stitch them together around the edges, then add decorative touches with extra felt and embroidery, as the mood takes you.

6. Sew a brooch back on at the back, and pin to your child's favourite coat.

Fab felt watch

Does anyone even wear a real watch anymore? With all the electronic devices carried about on our persons now (sporting in-built clock functions), they seem far less important than they once were. We only need watches to tell us when it's almost time for elevenses, anyway – right?

Make this purely decorative watch for little people from felt and remnant fabric when you're teaching them to read a clock. They can feel all grown-up and important, and use this as a reference without wandering about with the real thing.

'Clocks slay time …
only when the clock stops does time come to life.'

– William Faulkner

You will need

* ✳ Strip of felt, measuring about 20 cm long by 6 cm wide (8 × 2¹/₂ in)

* ✳ Strip of fabric, the same size

* ✳ Smaller pieces of felt in contrasting colours

* ✳ Small scissors

* ✳ Sewing needle and embroidery thread

* ✳ Chopstick

* ✳ Small amount polyester fibrefill or excess felt, for stuffing

* ✳ One large-ish press stud

Instructions

1. Take your smaller pieces of felt and cut out a watch face, border, dial and hands, using the photograph as a guide.

2. Sew into place in the middle of your larger strip of felt with embroidery thread, using a different-coloured thread on each piece if you can, to make it more interesting. Embroider lines where each of the numbers would be.

3. Place your felt and strip of fabric together, right sides facing each other, and use your scissors to cut slightly inwards around the section where your watch face ends and the straps begin, continuing along the straps to make them narrower than the watch face.

4. With a small seam allowance, sew the two pieces together, leaving a 5 cm (2 in) gap at one side of the face. Trim excess fabric from corners.

5. Turn right side out and use the chopstick to push out the corners – particularly at the ends of the straps.

6. Stuff lightly with polyfill or scraps of leftover felt.

7. Turn under the open edges of the gap and sew together with small overcasting stitches. Keep stitching in this manner around the outside until you're done; this will make the watch sit flat on the wrist.

8. Wrap the watch around your little one's arm, making a note of where the strap ends meet.

9. Sew each side of the press stud to the end of either strap.

10. Place on the wrist, snap together and send your little one on their way (not really) burdened by Old Father Time.

Keeping little hands busy

Cut a much larger clock face from felt as well as some numbers, and encourage your young one to put the numbers in the right spots. Attach with press-studs or sew a small button at each number position and make a simple slit in the numbers so they can be buttoned in place.

Keeping little hands busy

Kids love making pompoms! Cut some cardboard circles, show them how to wind the wool and watch them go. You might have to help with the last bit unless they're old enough to handle a needle, but they'll be transfixed by how wool-covered circles turn into a perfect, fluffy ball.

Pompom garlands

How can you not love a pompom or two? Or several, to be worn as a necklace? They're simply too fun, and will brighten up any child's outfit. Collect balls of brightly coloured wool whenever you see them to create a rainbow version, or rich reds and blues for understated winter style. These look great over a skivvy and tunic, or paired with opaque winter stockings, boots and a matching beanie (and not a little kooky). *Vive la différence!*

Your child will certainly stand out in the crowd, and their garland is likely to become the envy of the school yard (luckily, it's very easy for little friends to make their own, too).

You will need

* Several balls of wool in a riot of clashing colours

* Large tapestry needle

* Scissors

* Cardboard

* Tape measure

Instructions

1. Take your cardboard and cut out two circles, roughly the same size and shape as a doughnut, including the hole in the middle.

2. Put your two pieces of cardboard together, then take the end of your wool and tie a knot around the two pieces.

3. Cut a length of wool from a ball and re-wind it around two fingers, creating a smaller ball. This needs to fit through the hole in the middle of the cardboard, so keep it compact.

4. Wind your wool around and around the cardboard, pushing it through the hole in the middle, until you run out of wool.

5. Attach another length of wool to the end of the first piece and continue winding. As the hole in the middle gets smaller, you might find it easier to thread the end through with a tapestry needle.

6. When the hole has almost disappeared, take your scissors and start cutting through the wool at the outer edge of the doughnut. You will see the two pieces of cardboard in the middle. Use the space in between them as a guide to cut all the way around.

7. Pull apart the cardboard slightly and tie another piece of wool tightly around the middle of the doughnut shapes.

8. Remove the cardboard pieces on either side of the knot. Your pompom will spring into a ball shape. Carefully pull the wool into place, and trim the ball if it's a little lopsided, leaving a tail for tying the ball to the necklace. Your first pompom is complete.

9. Repeat Steps 1 to 8 until you have created at least five pompoms.

10. Now cut three lengths of wool, each measuring 50 cm (20 in).

11. Knot your three lengths of wool together at one end, then plait the threads together for the entire length. Tie a knot in the other end.

12. Now tie your pompoms to the plait, spaced evenly apart or all clustered together in the middle, depending on how they look.

13. When all the pompom balls are attached, tie in a bow around a little person's neck and get a kick out of how cute they look.

School treats

There is something very special about a child's first day at school. It's a milestone event, and usually much more emotional for mum and dad than the little one themselves. Who can forget their first school uniform or outfit? Carefully combed hair, a new backpack, well polished shoes and being posed outside the family home or school gates for a picture, filled with that heady feeling of excitement about all the adventures that lay ahead?

It's all very thrilling. This is your child's first real venture into the world – a chance to define themselves and forge friendships outside the family home. It's certainly character-building. I think it will be very interesting to watch them learning and taking so much in as the school year wears on, as well as growing both emotionally and in a social sense. Apart from us, yes, but closer towards the unique, independent individuals they are set to become. I don't want to wish Olive's life away, but I look forward to getting to know who she is by the choices she makes for herself in life. The first day of school is the first step towards their very own independence.

Remember tearing around the school yard, playing endless games like hopscotch and marbles and hide & seek? Colouring-in between the lines, learning your times tables and sharing secrets with your new best friends? Sports carnivals and school camp? Catching the bus and gold stars on your report cards? All this lies ahead, so it's important to take the time to enjoy it while it lasts. I like to think I will always have the time to ask Olive how her day was, and be there to listen to her latest news, thoughts and concerns, and work through any ups and downs. Wouldn't that be nice?

Make the following things for your child to take with them on this journey, and to remind them how much you love them, every single day. And involve them in your choices of fabric and colour, because they will be that much more likely to take pleasure in using them, and might even hold on to them for many years to come. You never know which items will become favourite things, but almost every one of these has the potential to become very precious indeed, with a little thought about your child's unique tastes and the things that make them especially happy.

Avoid Lost & Found

I have a friend whose son is so absent-minded, he's always losing things. One year, she had to buy him three pairs of the same school shoes because he kept leaving them on the bus or somewhere else after playing sport.

A place for everything and everything in its place, as they say. If you give things a home, and encourage kids to return things when they've stopped using them, you might (just might) be able to avoid all the disappearing acts. At least, you know the first place to look when items go AWOL.

Being someone with not-so-latent OCD tendencies, I love the idea of everything having a place where it belongs. I also think that if you designate certain places to store things, it's much easier to not just keep track of your possessions, but keep mess under control. It's deeply unfashionable to admit it, but a tidy home makes me happy.

Make some of the following items for storing children's bits and pieces for school. Fingers crossed, these will help them look after their belongings – a lesson it's never too early to learn, after all.

Special treasures pouch

This is for the bowerbirds among us.

I just loved keeping a stash of favourite things when I was little. Maybe some nice shells collected from the beach, or a feather, or pretty beads I'd been given as a gift. Remember that wonderful scene in the film *Amélie* where she returns a previous tenant in her home's childhood treasures tin to him? I think if I were faced with my own time capsule treasures stash, I might be taking a nostalgic stroll down memory lane also. That scene makes me smile so much, but then, so does the entire film.

Make one of these to store special things safely, from a charm bracelet to marbles, or to stop a brand-spanking-new Swiss army knife getting scratched. Pull the drawstrings tight to prevent precious items escaping, and loop through their belt so it can be carried around at all times. This will be both reassuring and very useful – maybe one day you can even pop it away somewhere safe for your child (treasures included) when they're no longer using it, and bring it out years later? Imagine what a lovely surprise that would be when they're grown-ups!

✳Tip
For a bigger or smaller pouch, all you need to do is create a larger or smaller circle for the size you need.

You will need

* Cotton fabric in a nice design
* Same amount plain cotton fabric
* A dinner plate or large pot
* Dressmaker's pencil
* Scissors
* About 2 m × 5 mm-wide (2^1/$_4$ yd × ^{1}/$_4$ in) ribbon
* Safety pin
* Sewing machine and thread
* Iron

Instructions

1. Lay one of your pieces of cotton out on the table, placing the dinner plate or large pot over it as a template.

2. Use the dressmaker's pencil to draw a line around the outside, and then cut out with your scissors.

3. Use your first circle as a pattern to cut another circle from the second fabric.

4. With right sides together, sew around the circumference of the circle, allowing a 1 cm (^{3}/$_8$ in) seam and leaving an opening of about 4 cm (1^1/$_2$ in) for turning.

5. Carefully clip across the seam allowance on the curves to ensure that the seam will sit flat, without puckers.

6. Turn the circles right side out and press, then fold in the raw edges and topstitch close to the outer edge, closing the opening at the same time.

7. Measure about 4 cm (1^1/$_2$ in) in from the outside edge of the circle, and use your chalk to mark a smaller circle inside the larger one.

8. Using the chalked line as a guide, sew around the smaller circle, and then sew another circle 1 cm (^{3}/$_8$ in) away from the first one, closer towards the centre.

9. On the outside of the bag, snip a tiny hole in the stitched casing you've just made, then snip another hole directly opposite the first one, on the other side of the circle. Take care that you snip through the outer layer of fabric only.

10. Cut your ribbon into two equal lengths. Using your safety pin as a guide, thread one length of ribbon through the casing until it re-emerges from where you began. Leaving about 5 cm (2 in) extra at each end of the ribbon, trim excess if necessary and tie in a knot.

11. Now repeat the above step with your second length of ribbon, but thread it through the other hole this time.

12. Pull the ends of the ribbon for the drawstrings, and pop treasures in before pulling completely closed. People will be more than a little curious about what's hidden inside.

Simple pencil case

Is your child a budding stationery fetishist? This one is for them. Yes, pencil cases are cheaper than chips and available in any supermarket, but that's exactly why I like the idea of making my own unique version. I adore oilcloth – it's especially useful for kids – and this is another idea for using a gorgeous design to maximum effect. Decorate the front if you like before you sew it all together, or just let the fabric do all the talking, as with this deliciously bright Mexican print.

And feel free to re-size if you need a smaller or larger version. A zippered case really works well to hold all manner of things nicely together and protected from spills. There's no reason why you couldn't create one for documents, or mum's makeup, or even a laptop with some added padding.

You will need

✳ Two 25 × 15 cm (10 × 6 in) rectangles of oilcloth

✳ 25 cm (10 in) zipper

✳ Sewing machine and thread

✳ Zipper foot

✳ Scissors

Instructions

1. With right sides together, stitch one side of the zipper to one of the longer edges of one oilcloth rectangle. Reverse a few times at either end for strength.

2. Sew the other rectangle to the other side of the zipper and reverse, just the same, at either end.

3. Open the zipper halfway, then, with right sides together, stitch the sides and bottom edges of the case together, making sure to sew rounded bottom corners.

4. Cut off the excess oilcloth at the corners, and turn the case right side out.

5. Pop in your child's pencils, textas, eraser and other bits and bobs before packing in their school bag for tomorrow's lessons.

Keeping little hands busy

Children can easily construct these themselves with a firm backstitch. Just sew the zip on the machine, and ask them to finish off the rest.

Super-kawaii book bag

Kawaii = Japanese for 'cute', and that's just what these mini-shopper bags are.

Make one for children to keep at the bottom of their school bags and it should come in handy for all sorts of things. Most importantly, it will be close by to store any extra homework or books they need to bring home occasionally.

It's good to teach children to carry about a reusable bag from an early age – think of all the plastic ones they'll be able to save over their lifetime if they start the habit young.

Have love (in the form of this beautiful handmade bag) and oh baby, we'll travel!

You will need

✳ Approximately 30 × 60 cm (12 × 24 in) soft cotton fabric in a cute design

✳ Two 45 × 7 cm (18 × 3 in) strips of a complementary fabric

✳ Measuring tape or ruler

✳ Scissors

✳ Sewing machine and thread

✳ Iron

✳ Bobble-headed pins

Instructions

1. Measure and cut two 30 cm (12 in) squares of fabric.

2. With *wrong* sides together and allowing 6 mm ($^1/_4$ in) seams, sew the squares together around three edges. Trim diagonally across the seam allowance on the lower corners and turn the bag inside out, so the right sides are now together. Press.

3. With *right* sides together, stitch around the sides and bottom edge again, this time allowing a 1 cm ($^3/_8$ in) seam allowance. (This double seam is called a French seam and gives a very strong, non-fray finish.)

4. Press under 6 mm ($^1/_4$ in) on the upper raw edge, then press under another 1 cm ($^3/_8$ in) and stitch this hem in place close to the inner fold, creating a neat opening edge. Leave the bag inside out at this stage.

5. Fold each strap in half lengthwise, right sides together, and stitch along the length, allowing a 1 cm ($^3/_8$ in) seam. Leave both short ends open.

6. With your iron, press the tube so that the seam you have just stitched runs down the centre of the strap (rather than on the edge) and press the seam allowance open.

7. Stitch across one short end on each strap. Trim diagonally across the seam allowance on the corners and turn the straps right side out.

8. Turn under the raw edges on the open end of each strap and press. Topstitch around all the edges of the straps, stitching close to the edge.

9. Pin the straps to the inside upper edge of the bag, equidistant from each side seam. Stitch the straps firmly in place, using two lines of stitching, for strength. Pop in some books and send your little one off on a reconnaissance mission to the local library.

Pretty utilitarian

There are so many boring things in life we all need to own. A brush and pan, an iron... socks. And when you need them immediately, they are absolutely the least fun things to spend money on. That is why, over the last decade, I have bought only two pairs of socks (and then, only when they could be worn on the outside of tights and shown off above a pair of leather boots, as well as a divine pair of knee-high Vivienne Westwood socks for a birthday gift). The rest I have shamelessly borrowed or stolen from my husband's drawers. And now my poor daughter is suffering from the mental block I've been plagued with for years: she has very few pairs of her own – on high rotation through the wash, of course – because I'd far rather be buying her tutus and beanies that make her look like a wild gypsy child than boring old socks!

There's always an opportunity to make home more personal by upgrading utilitarian items with something you find appealing, yet still useful. If it's recycled you can feel saintly to boot, and if children are involved in their making, they'll feel a connection to home every day, surrounded by their own very clever handiwork.

The only thing for it is to make dull (but nevertheless useful) items yourself, and to make them as attractive as possible in the process. I don't know if I'm up to designing a brush and pan (can I sew it together?), but how about a notebook cover, a lunch pail, a painting smock and an overnight bag for sleepovers? These I can manage (and so can you).

Gorgeous notebook cover

When I was little I was completely obsessed with stationery and still am. I totally broke one of the ten commandments (thou shalt not covet thy neighbour's goods) each day in school, wanting to chuck all my boring lead pencils away for a vast tin of rainbow-coloured Derwents, just like the set one of my schoolmates owned. I also loved candy-scented erasers, pretty pencil cases and anything with Japanese cartoons plastered all over it. Hmmm. My tastes have changed, but I still think it's better for everyday items to have a clever design. It just makes life more interesting when you use gorgeous things, *non*?

This is a very simple project and it's absolutely perfect to attempt with children. You might need to give them a little help to get started, but they will love decorating the cover to their own tastes, just as my friend's daughter Lucy did with the notebook behind mine on the following page.

Not only does a notebook cover protect books from wear and tear, it also provides the perfect opportunity to inject some individual flair in the playground. And it's reusable, so when the notebook is filled, you can replace it with a new one the same size.

You will need

✳ A notebook with a hard or stiff cardboard cover

✳ Enough fabric to cover notebook (and then some)

✳ Ruler

✳ Dressmaker's chalk

✳ Scissors

✳ Iron

✳ Sewing machine and thread (optional – you can also sew it together by hand)

✳ Smaller scraps of fabric and felt

✳ Buttons to decorate

✳ Embroidery needle and thread

Instructions

1. Lay your fabric, right side down, on a table and place your notebook, opened out, on top.

2. Use your ruler to measure 2 cm ($^3/_4$ in) from both the top and bottom edges, and 7 cm (3 in) from either side, for the flaps.

3. Cut out your rectangular piece of fabric and wrap around the notebook, and then use your iron to press flat the creases where the side flaps fold over.

4. Press under 6 mm ($^1/_4$ in) on all four raw edges of your rectangle and, using a contrasting sewing thread, topstitch close to the folded edge, creating a single hem.

5. Fold the flaps over flat where the creases are, and topstitch in place, following the hemline stitching.

6. Now you have your cover, you can play with small scraps of felt, fabric and buttons to create a unique cover design.

7. Taking care to avoid stitching through the flaps, sew on your bits and pieces with embroidery thread in bright, contrasting colours, going as crazy as you like with the embellishment.

8. Shimmy your notebook into the flaps at either side and flip closed.

Keeping little hands busy

Make the basic cover, then allow a small child to decorate, from drawing with fabric pens and gluing on shapes (and generally making a wonderful mess), to showing an older child how to sew on buttons, attach felt flowers and do simple embroidery stitches.

Soft lunch pails

This project really appeals to me – it's such a cute version of the standard rolled-up brown paper bag that a takeaway lunch often comes served in. I wish I'd had one of these for school when I was little, as my sandwiches always seemed to end up all over my bag, destroying books and jumpers (and lord knows what else), before I realised. With a soft lunch pail made from oilcloth, you can protect all the things in your child's schoolbag when things go a bit pear-shaped (providing they keep the top firmly rolled up and closed).

I first saw something similar to this on Etsy, but you can find them in quite a few places nowadays. They're dead easy to make, so go source some gorgeous oilcloth for your own favourite version. This one's made from Cath Kidston's delectable 'Round-up' fabric and a lime-green-and-white polka dot to contrast. I adore polka dots; they just seem to go with everything, don't they?

You will need

* Two 25 × 35 cm (10 × 14 in) pieces of oilcloth, for front and back
* 14 × 95 cm (5^1/$_2$ × 37^1/$_2$ in) piece contrasting oilcloth
* About 17 cm × 20 mm-wide (7 × ^{3}/$_4$ in) Velcro
* Sewing machine and thread
* 14 × 35 cm (5^1/$_2$ × 14 in) firm cardboard

Instructions

1. Take one of the front/back pieces of oilcloth and measure 9 cm (3^1/$_2$ in) down from the top (25 cm/10 in edge).

2. Place one half of the Velcro tape crosswise in the middle, and sew into place with your machine, following the outside edges of the tape and reversing a few times at the end for strength.

3. Take the other front/back piece and measure 2 cm (^{3}/$_4$ in) down from the top.

4. Place the other half of the Velcro tape crosswise in the middle and sew into place, as before.

5. With right sides together, line up one of your oilcloth front/back pieces with the long thin strip of contrast oilcloth in one corner.

6. Allowing a 6 mm (^{1}/$_4$ in) seam, sew along the edges until you reach the corner of the larger rectangle, then, with the needle in the fabric, lift your machine foot, swivel around to match the bottom edges, and keep sewing. Do this again when you reach the next corner, until the contrasting oilcloth is attached to the first piece on three sides.

7. Repeat Steps 5 and 6 with the other front/back piece of oilcloth to make your completed 'paper bag' shape.

8. Turn right side out.

9. Place the piece of cardboard in the bottom of the bag (I've used part of an old pizza box myself, if you can believe it), then roll the top of the bag down and secure in place with the Velcro strips.

'Keep it clean' painting smock

While I don't really adhere to the idea of saving certain clothes for special occasions (every day should be an event to dress up for!) I do think it's important to look after our favourite clothes when we're undertaking messy cooking or craft projects. Make this useful, pretty smock out of oilcloth and kit out Crafty Kids in an old men's shirt that's ready for the rag bag, with smock on top. Wearing both should give them enough coverage to prevent any food or painting mishaps seeping through to clean items underneath, and save you having to scrub them out in the wash. Now they're protected, encourage them to get stuck right in.

You could also consider making a smaller version of this smock for a toddler – the oilcloth is easy to hose down after particularly chaotic mealtimes.

You will need

✳ Tape measure

✳ Oilcloth to fit – 0.5 m ($^5/_8$ yd) should be more than enough

✳ Pen

✳ Scissors

✳ 25 mm-wide (1 in) bias binding

✳ Small plate or saucer

✳ Bobble-headed pins

✳ 4 cm ($1^1/_2$ in) strip Velcro tape

Instructions

1. Measure across the widest part of your child's chest, from armpit to armpit. Add an extra 4 cm ($1^1/_2$ in) to this measurement, for ease. Measure also the child's length, from shoulder to knees.

2. Lay out your oilcloth, wrong side facing upwards, and mark a rectangle shape to fit your width-by-length measurements. Rule a line down the centre of this rectangle, from top to bottom.

3. Enlarge the pattern piece for the smock Front (on page 240) until the width of the chest measurement just fits in one half of your rectangle. The A-line edge of the pattern piece will extend beyond the edge of your ruled rectangle. Trace around the pattern piece, then flip it over, along the centre front line, and trace the other side, giving you one complete Front.

4. Enlarge the pattern piece for the smock Back to the same proportions as the Front and trace two outlines onto the wrong side of the oilcloth, flipping the pattern to get two mirror-image Backs.

5. Use a small plate to trace a half-circle onto the oilcloth for a Pocket.

6. Now cut out all your smock pieces on the traced lines.

7. With right sides together, pin the Back sections of the smock to the Front at both shoulders, and then stitch the seams in place.

8. Take your bias binding, fold it over the armhole edges of the smock and topstitch in place.

9. Now, with right sides together, sew the Front and Back pieces to each other at the side seams.

10. Starting at the bottom right-hand corner, sew your bias binding into place, following around the entire edge of the smock until you get back to your starting place. Cut off any excess binding, fold under the raw end and sew into place, reversing a few times at the end.

11. Sew binding around the Pocket, folding it neatly at the corners.

12. Pin the Pocket to the front of the smock, and sew around the curved edge, following the binding stitching line.

13. Stitch the Velcro strips onto the back flaps. Now, get painting!

An overnight bag

Every child reaches an age where they start to have sleepovers at friends' houses. The first time can be quite daunting, what with unusual foods and rules and sleeping between unfamiliar sheets. Make this fun gift to help them relish the hurdle – cake always helps promote bravery, after all!

This simple felt bag is the perfect overnighter. Pack with pyjamas, a change of clothes and your child's toothbrush for sleepovers. Decorate with a slice of cake or something else to denote special occasions (a pile of sweets, perhaps, or a plane?), plant a swift kiss on each cheek and wave them off at the gate. And don't be thrown by the tears (I'm talking about your own).

Now order in pizza or make a reservation for a nice meal out with your other half or some friends. Go on, otherwise it's such a wasted opportunity!

You will need

✳ Two pieces of felt: 45 × 114 cm (18 × 45 in), for the bag, and 8 × 25 cm (3¹/₄ × 10 in), for the strap

✳ Same amount of cotton print, for bag and strap lining

✳ Smaller pieces of felt for the cake

✳ Small scraps of fabric for the plate, spoon and cream

✳ Scissors

✳ Sewing machine and thread

✳ Two kilt pins

✳ Iron

Instructions

1. Lay your larger pieces of felt and cotton together, right sides facing each other, and sew around all four edges – allowing a 6 mm (¹/₄ in) seam and leaving open a gap of about 10 cm (4 in).

2. Turn right side out through opening and press. Turn under the edges of the opening and topstitch around the outer edge of the whole piece, securing the opening at the same time.

3. Lay the piece on your work surface with the felt side facing up. To create the body of the bag, fold up the bottom edge by about 38 cm (15 in), bringing the felt sides together. Starting at the top, stitch the sides together, finishing the seam about 8 cm (3 in) from the bottom fold.

4. Now bring the bottom fold up to meet the bottom of the seam, squashing the bottom up on itself like a milk carton. Stitch along both sides to give a boxed corner.

5. Repeat the above step on the remaining bottom corner, and turn bag right side out.

6. Take your smaller strips of felt and cotton and lay them together, right sides facing each other. Allowing a 6 mm (¹/₄ in) seam, sew together around three sides, leaving one of the shorter ends open.

7. Turn right side out and press. Turn under the open edges and topstitch close to the outer edge of the whole piece, securing the opening at the same time.

8. On the back of the bag, at the point where the flap folds over the front, measure 14 cm (5¹/₂ in) in from each side and pin the ends of the handle at these points, so that it sits like a small loop. Stitch firmly in place with a small rectangle of stitching at each end.

9. Using the shapes on page 239, cut out your pieces of felt and fabric and arrange them on the flap of the bag.

10. Set your machine to a zigzag stitch and sew the pieces into place around the edges, one layer at a time, until you have built up the completed motif. You can also sew by hand with embroidery thread if you prefer.

11. Use the kilt pins to secure the flap when the bag is full. Chop chop, off they go.

Playground fun

I don't know if it's the done thing anymore, but I remember dress-up days from little school, where we got kitted out in costumes as our favourite fictional character and formed a Book Day Parade that wound its way through the grounds and ended with prizes in the assembly hall. One year, I came as Anne of Green Gables, paired with my best friend Diana, Anne's 'kindred spirit'. We bought cans of spray-on hair colour from the chemist and I was transformed into a carrot-coloured redhead for the day, while my poor, naturally fair friend looked like a Goth, with her long black locks (or 'raven tresses', as Anne would have called them). Sadly, we did not win any prizes. I think that went to The Cat in the Hat.

I remember recess and lunchtimes as very fun events on most days, even when it was pouring with rain outside and we were stuck in the classroom, eating sandwiches at our desks. We devised elaborate games which usually involved imagining ourselves as the characters in popular films or television shows and came up with unconvincing plot deviations.

Let the games begin with these finger puppets and the little piggy face mask included here. And yes, I am officially obsessed with felt.

Punch & Judy finger puppets

I have an admission to make: I find Punch & Judy shows amusing. There was a time when I had no sense of humour about the very un-PC spectacle of Punch, the gnarled hunchback, beating his wife Judy over the head with a stick (around the time I was enrolled in Women's Studies at University). I may even have wandered off, a bit disgusted, at the fair. But now they make me laugh; I really enjoy it, for the tradition of the puppet booth more than anything. It's so Olde Worlde. So analogue! Punch would take your hand-held video game and smash it to smithereens, don't you think? Haaaaiii-yaaah! Take that, Tomb Raider.

Make these finger puppets for your dear wee child and watch them become very exuberant. Hand-to-hand combat is so much fairer than fighting with guns, anyway.

You will need

✳ Red, beige, pink, blue, grey and brown felt

✳ A wooden satay stick

✳ Embroidery needle and thread

✳ Scissors

Instructions

1. Use the the patterns on page 237 to cut out the basic shapes of both Punch and Judy from the red and pink felt respectively. You will need two layers of each colour per finger puppet.

2. Now cut out their faces, hands and the centre of Judy's flower from beige felt, Judy's curls from the grey felt, Judy's flower and Punch's shirt lapels from blue felt and Punch's stick from brown felt (you will need two layers for the stick).

3. Lay your smaller felt pieces over the basic shapes of Punch and Judy, putting the second layer of each aside for the moment.

4. Using tiny running stitch, sew on their faces, hands, hair, flower and lapels first, and then the expressions on their faces, including their rosy cheeks, chin and nose.

5. Now place the top layer on the backing and stitch together, leaving a hole for little fingers to poke through at the bottom.

6. Put the remaining pieces of brown felt for the stick together and stitch around three sides with embroidery thread, leaving one of the shorter sides open.

7. Trim the satay stick to fit inside the felt tube, and stitch closed at the open short end.

8. Stitch the stick to Punch's hand and pop another few stitches in where the stick meets the bottom of his shirt. Now you're ready to get punching.

Keeping little hands busy

These tiny puppets require an adult level of dexterity, but encourage children to make their own hand puppets from an old sock. Depending on their age, they can either glue or sew bits and pieces, such as felt, buttons and wool, to create a vast array of animals – or even a monster.

Little piggy face mask

Never mind little savages, kids can be real animals sometimes (well technically, they are, but you know what I mean). Is yours being a little piggy today? You decide.

Make this mask from felt, fab fake fur or fleece. It really is quite a lot of fun to construct and looks so much better than the store-bought, 'Made in China' variety. It also makes an excellent gift or fancy dress mask for a party, and children will enjoy hiding behind their four-legged alter-ego, making 'oink' sounds at you. Now, this is no excuse for them to turn their rooms into a pig pen.

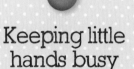

Keeping little hands busy

While you're busy with the felt mask, little helpers could be making their own masks from paper plates. Cut out the eye holes, then let them draw and glue on scraps of felt, fabric and paper. Staple a piece of narrow elastic to the sides to hold the mask in place.
What fun!

You will need

✳ Felt in pink and cream

✳ Cotton fabric for backing

✳ Hat elastic to fit

✳ Dressmaker's chalk

✳ Pure wool stuffing

✳ Scissors

✳ Needle and thread or sewing machine

✳ Embroidery needle and thread

Instructions

1. Using the shapes on page 234, trace and cut one Face, two Ears, one Nose and one Snout, from pink felt, adding 6 mm (¼ in) seam allowance all round, when cutting. From backing fabric, cut one Face and two Ears, adding seam allowance. From cream felt, cut two Inner Ears and two Nostrils (without seam allowance).

2. Use running stitch to stitch the felt Inner Ears to the centre of each cotton Ear. With right sides together and allowing 6 mm (¼ in) seams, sew the Ears together in pairs, leaving the lower edge open. Trim the seam allowance, turn the ears right side out and press.

3. With right sides together and raw edges matching (make sure the inner ear will be facing the front), baste the ears to the top of the felt mask, folding in the outer edge a little on each ear as you baste.

4. Wrap the mask around the child's face to work out how much elastic you will need (it should be lightly stretched to give a snug fit), then cut elastic to this length. Make a large knot at each end of the elastic, then catch the knots in place with a couple of stitches on each side of the front of the mask.

5. With right sides together, sew the Face and backing pieces together around the outer edge, allowing 6 mm (¼ in) seams and securing the ears and ends of the elastic in the seam. Leave an opening of about 5 cm (2 in) in the bottom edge, for turning.

6. Turn right side out and press. Turn under the raw edges of the opening and slipstitch opening closed.

7. Lay the mask over the top part of your child's face to get an idea where their eyes are. Mark gently and cut out the eye holes from each mask through the two layers of fabric.

8. Use a needle and thread to stitch around the eyes with small, firm stitches, rolling under the raw edge of the backing as you stitch.

9. Stitch the Nostrils to the Nose with running stitch. Stitch the short ends of the Snout together, then stitch the Nose to one end of the Snout, right sides together. Fill the snout with stuffing, and stitch to the front of the mask.

10. Add any other facial details, as desired.

11. Little ones are now ready to head off to market... or run (weeeee!) all the way home.

Get out in the garden

When the natives are getting restless and it's simply too nice outside to stay in, encourage the kids to go out in the garden to play.

It's so much healthier for children to be enjoying fresh air and vitamin D from a little sun anyway, rather than being plonked in front of the television. They can run around, burning off all that childish energy so they'll be more active, for a start – one of the first steps to combating some of the problems of our increasingly sedentary lifestyles – because who can sit still when there's so much to see and touch and explore?

As a kid, I remember having the most fabulous tree house (just a wooden ledge, really) at the top of our backyard jacaranda tree. One of my sweetest memories is taking time out to sit up there with a book or game, and maybe a slice of something nice, then peering out through the purple flowers at the hilly suburb below, laid out like a map before me. Children love cubby-houses and their own private places, so carve out a space for them by building a tree house or mini-shack, and let them decorate it themselves. Provide room to let their imaginations run wild and supply any materials you can to stimulate it: paint, chalk, pens, paper, scissors, glue and notebooks. Or give them the equipment for simple outdoors games like hopscotch, soccer, cricket or croquet and leave them to it.

The garden is the first place your child will discover the beauty and intricacy of nature (or the park if you're an inner-city apartment-dweller). Even a window box or small balcony garden can provide a microcosm for them to study, up-close-and-personal, and they can while away hours tending to the plants and flowers.

We have a wisteria plant in a large pot under our back patio. I was watering it one day when I noticed the largest praying mantis I'd ever seen. He had huge, googly eyes, and was the exact shade of acid-bright green as the new leaves and shoots on our wisteria, and seemed to have been studying me long before I noticed he was there. Olive was too little then, but I couldn't wait to have a child big enough to run and grab, to say, 'Look – let me introduce you to our new friend.'

Repeat after me, in tones of appropriate wonderment: *nature's amazing!*

Grow to love

Making children familiar with the plants and insects literally living in your own backyard will foster an appreciation for nurturing things from very early on. Following the shortish life cycle of plants is the perfect way to explain life and death to a young child, and you might as well start this conversation young, if ever so gently. It will also teach them to be still for a moment while they contemplate the delicate beauty of water veins on a leaf, or the ladybird alighted there.

I can't think of a better way to show children the bounty of nature than by helping them plant and grow flowers, such as daffodils or violets, and delicious things to eat, like baby carrots and lettuce. And by teaching them to remove unwanted guests, such as aphids and snails, by hand rather than with a spray of nasty pesticides. The patience and involvement required will teach them incredibly valuable skills for life, and hopefully turn them into the kind of adult who actively thinks about our reliance on nature. After all, we have the trees to thank for the air we breathe, and soil for all our food. Don't assume they will garner this information in school. How can we rely on them to care for the future of the planet and everything on it, if we don't teach them the basics first in the most important place of all: the home?

Seriously lovely wide-brimmed sunhat

I love a big, floppy sunhat to wear in the garden or whenever I'm outside for extended periods of time, but they're particularly important for little ones with their sensitive skin and to protect them from burning. I think it's very sensible that schools now enforce the rule of children popping one on before they're let outside to play at lunchtime or recess each day. I wish I'd grown up in such a skin-cancer aware environment myself.

You can't really have too many, either. Keep one of these sunhats in the car for spontaneous trips to the park on a hot day, one next to the front door on a hook, and one in the bottom of their backpacks, just so you (and they) never find yourselves short. They'll thank you for it many years later, when their skin is healthy and far less lined or damaged than their sun-loving contemporaries.

You will need

✳ 0.4 m × 112 cm-wide ($1/2$ yd × 44 in) sturdy fabric with print on both sides (see Tip on page 150)

✳ 1.7 m × 15 mm-wide ($1^7/8$ yd × $5/8$ in) grosgrain ribbon

✳ Approximately 1.4 m × 25 mm-wide ($1^1/2$ yd × 1 in) bias binding

Instructions

1. The pattern pieces are printed on page 243. Trace them onto paper, then use your photocopier to enlarge them to the correct size. The printed pattern at correct size will fit a head up to about 49 cm (19 in) in circumference. If you want to enlarge or reduce the pattern, do so until the length of the full Crown section is the correct measurement for the circumference of the head (including 2 cm ($3/4$ in) seam allowance), and make sure that you enlarge or reduce the remaining pieces in the same ratio.

2. To cut the Brim and Crown, fold the fabric in two, right sides together, and pin the straight edges of the Brim pattern piece and one straight edge of the Crown along the fold of the fabric, then cut out. Open out the fabric to a single layer and cut one Top. All pieces include 1 cm ($3/8$ in) seam allowance.

3. With right sides together and allowing a 1 cm ($3/8$ in) seam, stitch the short edges of the Crown together. Trim one edge of the seam allowance back to 3 mm ($1/8$ in). Press under the raw edge of the remaining seam allowance and press it over the top of the trimmed seam allowance. Topstitch the pressed edge in place – this will completely enclose the raw edges of both seam allowances, leaving a very neat seam.

4. With right sides together, stitch the Top to the Crown. Trim the seam allowance and neaten with a zigzag stitch.

5. Fold the Brim into quarters and mark the quarter-circle points with a pin. Do the same for the Crown. With right sides together and matching quarter-circle points, pin and sew Brim to the lower edge of the Crown. Snip across the seam allowance towards the seam at 2 cm ($3/4$ in) intervals, taking care not to snip into the seam itself.

6. For the brim band, cut a length of grosgrain ribbon that will fit around the inside of the Brim, adding about 2.5 cm (1 in) for overlap. Cut remaining ribbon in half for ties.

7. Baste a ribbon tie to the brim seam on each side of the hat. Starting at the centre back seam, pin the brim band to the inside of the hat, positioning the lower edge of the ribbon along the seam line. Stitch the ribbon in place close to the edge, catching the raw ends of the ribbon ties in the seam and turning under the raw edge in a neat overlap when you get back to the beginning. The ribbon hides the raw edges of the brim seam and prevents the seam from rolling outwards. The stitching will show on the outside of the hat as a neat line of topstitching close to the brim seam. The remaining, upper edge of the ribbon is not stitched.

8. Starting at the centre back of the Brim, pin and stitch the bias binding over the raw edge of the Brim, folding under the raw edge of the binding neatly at the join. All done – you have youself a sunhat.

Keeping little hands busy

Hats are sometimes hard to keep on little ones' heads, not least because they tire of feeling constricted. Keep them at hand while making this sunhat to check it fits properly, and ask their opinion on all fabric and ribbon choices.

You could even let them create an accessory or two to decorate the brim to their tastes.

*Tip

My fabric was the same on both sides, making it easy to cut a single Brim. If you are using a fabric that has a right and wrong side, you should cut two Brims and baste them to each other, wrong sides facing, then proceed with the instructions as though they were a single piece. With very lightweight fabric, you might want to simply make two complete hats and use one to line the other before binding the edge.

Nifty kneeler

Apart from little faces, the next most important thing to keep safe is tiny knees from bruises, scrapes and small pointy things while children are helping you in the garden. Make this kneeler from a sturdy, preferably waterproof, material with a durable canvas strap for the handles. You'll find the weeding is not even half as tedious with good accessories.

I like this green gingham oilcloth for the garden, which can either be hosed or wiped down when your little one is finished, and left to dry on the back step. You can also use an old tarpaulin if you have one, or one of those cheap plastic laundry sacks usually found in the Chinatown of every major city on Earth. I've paired it with straps unpicked from the bottom seam of a French feed sack because I know they'll last the distance, and the murky colour means they won't show grubby dirt stains – definitely something to consider.

You will need

* 42 × 66-cm (16^1/$_2$ × 26-in) thick waterproof fabric (oilcloth or similar)

* 60 × 5 cm-wide (24 × 2 in) sturdy woven strap, for the handles

* Sewing machine and thread

* Denim needle

* Pins

* Polyester fibrefill

Instructions

1. Fold your fabric in half crosswise, right sides together, so that it measures 42 × 33 cm (16^1/$_2$ × 13 in).

2. Allowing about 1 cm (^{3}/8 in) for your seam, sew the long edges together, reversing a few times at either end for strength. Repeat with a line of zigzag stitching. You should have a tube, about the same size as one of those furry hand-warmer things the Russians wear in Cold War-era American films like *Gorky Park*.

3. Turn your tube right side out, and fold the edges under by 1 cm (^{3}/8 in).

4. Cut your strap in half, giving two 30 cm (12 in) pieces.

5. Measure 5 cm (2 in) in from each side at one end of your tube, slip the ends of one strap between the folded edges and pin in place for a handle. Make sure the strap is folded only once in the middle rather than twisted around a few times, so it sits like the handle in the picture.

6. Topstitch across the folded edges of the tube, reversing a few times at either side and as you go over each end of the strap.

7. Stuff the cushion with fibrefill, leaving enough room at the other end to get the hem under the sewing machine's foot.

8. Repeat Steps 5–6 to complete the other end of your kneeler. Easy peasy.

A trug for pesky weeds

The popular garden designer Paul Bangay once said in an interview that the thing he hates most is being asked to create a low-maintenance garden, because there's no such thing. I take heart from this when I'm fretting about the dandelions that seem to have appeared out of nowhere amongst a patch of star jasmine, the suddenly wild appearance of our cherry blossom tree or the scorched gardenias after a few days of unseasonable heat. It's not very smart to admit, but I have to say I get quite a thrill bringing the garden back from the brink of death with a few days of TLC after a short period of neglect.

When the weeds are out of control, supply willing helpers with this handy trug to match the Nifty Kneeler – you'll feel on top of things before you've even started. I've made this long and thin version because your family might be clever enough to be cutting long-stemmed blooms or collecting vegetables from the garden instead of weeds. Needless to say, the main duty of ours is holding the latter as we shuffle about tidying things up.

You will need

* 70 × 70 cm (28 × 28 in) oilcloth or similar (see the previous project for some creative alternatives)

* Same amount of hessian, for your lining (a recycled feed sack is actually perfect)

* 50 × 5 cm-wide (20 × 2 in) sturdy woven strap, for the handle

* Sewing machine and thread

* Denim needle

* Pins

Instructions

1. Fold your oilcloth in half so it measures 70 × 35 cm (28 × 14 in) and, with rights sides together and allowing 1 cm (3/8 in) seams, stitch the shorter sides together, leaving the upper edge open.

2. To create wide boxed corners, fold the lower corner into a point so that the side seam is centred at the apex and aligned with the bottom seam. Measure 10 cm (4 in) down the seam from the apex and rule a straight line across the corner at this point. Sew across the ruled line, securing the stitching firmly at each end. Make another line of stitching close to the first for strength. Trim off the corner, leaving 1 cm (3/8 in) seam allowance.

3. Repeat Step 2 for the opposite corner. The bottom of your trug should measure about 20 cm (8 in) across.

4. Repeat Steps 1–3 with the hessian lining, but leave a 15 cm (6 in) opening just below the upper edge in one side seam during Step 3.

5. Turn the outer bag right side out, measuring and marking the centre point on each opening edge of the bag.

6. Pin the raw ends of the strap to these points on the outside of the bag, allowing about 5 cm (2 in) on each end of the strap to extend above the raw edge of the bag. Machine-baste the straps in position.

7. Slip the lining bag over the outer bag, right sides together, aligning side seams and upper opening edges.

8. Allowing a 1 cm (3/8 in) seam, sew right around the upper opening edge, sandwiching the straps in the seam as you stitch.

9. Now pull the whole thing right side out through the hole that you left in the lining side seam.

10. Turn under raw edges on each side of opening and stitch the opening closed by hand or machine. Push lining down into the bag.

11. Now topstitch around the upper edge of the bag, stitching 3 mm (1/8 in) from the edge.

12. Finally, to reinforce the strap ends, topstitch a 5 cm (2 in) square on top of where the strap is inserted into the bag, stitching through all layers and stitching diagonally in both directions across the square for extra strength.

Cloud spotting

We often forget how easy it is to re-balance ourselves by indulging in even a short stint of peaceful time alone, particularly in nature. Like most people, I always find time for my favourite activities – being with family and friends, browsing markets, reading and making things – but will go months at a time before remembering to sit down and share a meditative few minutes or longer with myself. This is just as important (if not more so) for children. They need time to imagine and dream – it will give them much better attention spans as adults, and a foundation of calm in tricky situations over the course of their lives.

I was much better at letting my mind go truly blank when I was a child. We lived opposite a rambling park for a while, and I used to lie down in its lush carpet of clover and gaze at the dusky sky on summer evenings. With the drone of bees and cicadas providing an Om-like soundtrack, I felt a profound lightness – a feeling of suspension – and would often rouse myself from an open-eyed, sleep-like state an hour later. Similarly, I've captured that same fleeting feeling, lying on a beach sand dune at dawn, conscious only of the sky slowly lightening around me and the wind whistling through the scrubby grass by my ears.

Water flowing in a stream, waves crashing at the beach, rain pattering down on a tin roof, wind rustling through leaves in the trees, insects providing a monotonous orchestra or even a cat's steady purr: these are all sounds to relax the mind, body and spirit. But keep your eyes open. Gaze at the sky for help; the brain can't comprehend what a tiny speck of insignificance you are in relation to its vast and ancient existence. It should be enough to make your thoughts quiet and shut down entirely... even for just a few moments. Then face the time ahead with a renewed feeling of peace.

Let's go fly a kite...

It's easier to achieve a sense of relaxation with props. For some people, this means soaking in a warm bath; while others exercise, play a game or go fishing to feel the knots of tension unwind themselves. Children are often open to trying new things, so help them find their own favourite relaxation activity by introducing them to many different pastimes when they're young.

Our very dear friends from England, Hamish and Katie, gave us a kite once as a Christmas gift. It's actually a para-kite (a cross between a paraglider and a kite) so it's huge and quite capable of lifting you off your feet in a strong gust of wind. It requires ample space to get going so we don't use it often, but it's a real thrill – and a very childish sort of pleasure – to watch it lift off the ground and be able to keep it in the air. We used to love flying it in London's Richmond Park, although the sound it made when it crashed to the ground always scared the deer and we'd feel guilty for starting a mini-stampede.

The feeling you get – mainly achieved from the skill and concentration required to keep a kite in the air – is very close to mindlessness. Enjoy total inner peace while your kite soars, even just for those few moments you are able to keep it gliding, airborne, through the clouds.

Here's a kite for you to create with your young ones: my neighbours David and Anna made it with three-year-old daughter Ruby in less than an hour, and enjoyed working on it as a family project.

Up to the highest heights...

Keeping little hands busy

If your child can tie a bow, he or she can tie all the bows for the kite's tail. Smaller assistants might like to decorate the paper (or even plain calico) with paint or felt-tip pens before you cover the frame.

You will need

* Two lengths of fine wooden dowel, measuring 88 cm (34^1/$_2$ in) and 1 m (39^1/$_2$ in) respectively

* Craft glue

* Ball of twine

* Stanley knife

* Scissors

* 100 × 100 cm (39^1/$_2$ × 39^1/$_2$ in) sheet of paper, calico or oilcloth

* Ribbons, for the kite's tail

Instructions

1. Place the shorter piece of wooden dowel horizontally across the longer one to make a cross shape.

2. Dab a spot of glue in the place where both pieces intersect, and secure by winding the twine tightly around a number of times, tying a knot when finished. This will be your kite's frame.

3. Use your Stanley knife to notch the ends of each piece of dowel so there's a space for the twine to sit inside the grooves comfortably. Now wrap the twine around the edges of the cross frame until it sits taut, in a diamond shape.

4. When you reach the top and bottom of the vertical dowel, tie a small knot in the twine to create a loop on each, and then tie the end of the twine into a knot. Snip off any excess twine.

5. Lay the paper or oilcloth out flat and place the kite frame over it. Cut around its diamond shape, allowing a 3 cm (1^1/$_4$ in) margin.

6. Fold the edges of the paper over the string frame and glue flat against the underside of the kite, cutting out a space with your scissors to allow the looped twine to remain uncovered at each end.

7. Measure a piece of twine 120 cm (47 in) long, and tie each end to the loops at either end of the frame. This is the kite's bridle.

8. Measure another piece of twine about 2 m (79 in) long, and make a tail by tying the twine to the loop at the bottom of the kite (also used to secure the bridle).

9. Tie your ribbons in small bows roughly every 15 cm (6 in) along the length of twine. This is your tail.

10. Take the remaining ball of twine, and secure the end to the middle of the bridle.

11. Make a trip to your local park, encourage your child to hold onto the ball of twine and unravel it while you move a good few metres away. Carefully launch it into the air, pull back, and watch it fly!

Perfect picnic blanket

It's useful to have a picnic blanket in the back of the car for times when you find yourself out and about on a beautiful day. Sometimes, it's much nicer to grab a coffee or sandwich and sit in a nearby park rather than inside a noisy café. And it's blissful, spreading yourself out with the papers to relax while the kids tear around, wearing themselves out. Small babies also love lying on the ground under a tree. The movement of the wind through the leaves above will keep them fascinated for ages.

Use a picnic blanket in your garden as well, when the grass is soggy, to delineate a patch for you or the children to lie back and spot clouds.

Make this waterproof version from a recycled bed blanket. I found a gorgeous, heather-coloured wool blanket in a charity store for $5 not long ago. Seriously moth-eaten around the edges, I cut fabric from the relatively undamaged middle and backed it with fabulous purple and orange-patterned oilcloth. I've also inserted a thin layer of batting to make it extra soft and comfortable to sit on. Stitch around the outside by hand for a wonderfully handmade-looking finish, and simply tie a ribbon or twill tape around and in a bow to make it extra-easy to store.

You will need

* An old blanket (if it has marks or holes, just cut around them)
* Oilcloth
* Thin wool batting
* Scissors
* Pins
* Sewing machine and thread
* Denim needle
* Wool, to use as thread
* Large sewiang needle
* Approximately 1 m (39 in) ribbon

Instructions

1. Cut your blanket, oilcloth and batting to the same size. This will depend on the amount of undamaged blanket you have to work with; here, I've used roughly 100 × 150 cm (39 × 59 in).

2. Place your blanket and oilcloth backing together, right sides facing each other, and lay the batting on top of the blanket.

3. Secure all three pieces together with pins, spaced at roughly 10 cm (4 in) intervals.

4. Use your machine to sew around three sides with a seam allowance of about 1 cm (^{3}/8 in). Leave one of the shorter sides open.

5. To reduce bulk, trim the seam allowance of the batting back almost to the stitching line. Turn the blanket right side out, enclosing the batting between the two outer layers.

6. Fold under the seam allowance on the open edges, then use your wool thread to sew the edges closed with a running stitch.

7. Keep sewing with a running stitch around the remaining three edges, re-threading when you need to and making sure any knotted ends are on the underside of the blanket.

8. Fold your blanket in half lengthwise with the oilcloth facing outwards, then roll it up nice and tight, like you would a sleeping bag. Tie your ribbon around it with a bow, to keep it rolled, and tuck away for later use.

'Caravan of love' cubby house

Remember weddings and other important events when you were a child, when all you wanted to do was sneak under a trestle table with siblings or new friends and play a game, rather than sit still through the formality of speeches or dinner or watching people on the dance floor? I do.

I'm completely enamoured with the idea of this. Don't you think it's such a cute solution to turn a table into a mini-caravan for little ones to enjoy? And with oilcloth on the top, you can just as easily serve lunch or afternoon tea on the tabletop, while wee faces poke out from the windows beneath.

Set this up at your next party or barbecue either inside or out in the garden, and watch the kiddies retreat for some much-needed play or imagination time during the festivities.

You will need

* Oilcloth
* Calico or other sturdy fabric
* Clear plastic, for windows
* 0.45 m × 112 cm-wide ($1/2$ yd × 44 in) print fabric, for curtains
* 2 m × 20 mm-wide (2 yd × $3/4$ in) grosgrain ribbon, for curtain ties
* 1 m ($1 1/8$ yd) red mini pompom braid, for windows
* Blue mini pompom braid, for trim
* Print fabrics, for appliqué trim
* Sewing thread and needle
* Ruler and felt-tip pen
* Pinking shears, optional
* Ribbon, for ties, optional
* Suitable table with ample space underneath

Instructions

1. The amount of fabric and oilcloth you need for your cubby will depend on the size of the table that the cubby is to fit over.

2. Using the diagram on page 238 as a guide, measure the width (A), the length (B) and the height (C) of your table, allowing a little extra for ease. Make a note of these measurements.

3. For the Sides of the cubby, measure and cut two rectangles from calico, each B + 2 cm ($3/4$ in) × C + 3 cm ($1 1/4$ in).

4. For the Back of the cubby, cut one rectangle from calico or other sturdy fabric, A + 2 cm ($3/4$ in) × C + 3 cm ($1 1/4$ in).

5. For the Front Flaps of the cubby, cut two rectangles from oilcloth, each $1/2$A + 3 cm ($1 1/4$ in) × C + 1 cm ($3/8$ in). I cut along the bottom edge of each of my Flaps with pinking shears, but this isn't strictly necessary, as oilcloth doesn't fray.

6. For the Top of the cubby, cut one rectangle from oilcloth, A + 2 cm ($3/4$ in) × B + 2 cm ($3/4$ in).

7. Take your two Front Flaps and use your ruler and felt-tip pen to rule up a 24 cm ($9 1/2$ in) square in the centre of each rectangle, starting 16 cm ($6 1/4$ in) down from the upper edge. Carefully cut out and remove these squares to make windows in your two Front Flaps.

8. Cut two squares of clear plastic, 1 cm ($3/8$ in) larger all round than the window openings. Position the clear plastic squares behind the window openings and sew in place around the edges – you can sew all four edges, or just sew the top and bottom, leaving the sides open for a little ventilation.

9. To make the curtains, cut your print fabric in half crosswise, giving two rectangles, 45 × 56 cm (18 × 22 in). Press under 1 cm ($3/8$ in) double hems on both short sides and one long edge and stitch in place. Pin a series of evenly-spaced pleats across the unhemmed edge so that curtain will fit into the window space. Adjust pleats as necessary, then baste across upper edge to hold. Stitch the pleated edge of the curtain behind the window opening along the upper edge.

10. Cut pieces of mini pompom braid to fit along the upper and lower edges of the window and sew in place.

11. Cut your grosgrain ribbon in half and tie one piece around each curtain, finishing each with a cheerful bow.

12. Lap your completed Front Flaps over one another a little at the centre front until they measure exactly the same width as the calico Back rectangle. Baste with a few stitches at the top to hold the overlapped edges together.

13. Press under 1 cm ($3/8$ in) on one A + 2 cm ($3/4$ in) edge of Back, then press under another 1 cm ($3/8$ in) and stitch hem in place.

14. With right sides together and allowing 1 cm ($3/8$ in) seams, stitch the Back to one end of the Top, then stitch the Front Flaps to the other end.

15. Press up and stitch a 1 cm ($3/8$ in) double hem on the lower edge of each of the Sides (as for the Back).

16. Decorate the Sides, as you wish, with cut-outs from print fabric. I used large heart shapes cut from a red polka dot fabric, and also some flowers cut from a large floral print design. Appliqué your pieces in place with a zigzag stitch.

17. With right sides together and allowing 1 cm ($3/8$ in) seams, stitch the Sides in place along the side and top edges. Yay – you're almost done!

18. Cut a piece of mini pompom braid to fit around the side and back edges of the top (and the front too, if you like!) and stitch this in place to the seam line by hand.

19. If you want to, stitch a pair of ribbon ties to the Front Flaps.

20. Pop your completed cubby over the top of the table and have a cup of tea while your little ones play away to their heart's content.

✳ Tip

You can, of course, make the entire cubby from sturdy fabrics or calico rather than oilcloth, but remember to add extra seam allowance for hems on opening edges and around the windows.

Bath time

It's so easy to amass quite a lot of junk and unnecessary debris when you have kids – especially in the bathroom (my one-time sanctuary, where I used to spend hours soaking in near-scalding water reading the latest issue of *Vogue*, and now barely get three minutes to myself for a quick shower).

We've tried to order and keep the spreading mess of toys to a minimum elsewhere in our home, but it's nice for children to have lots of playthings, such as a collection of rubber ducks or sailing boats to keep them splashing about happily in the bath for ages. That's why we keep quite a lot of toys in there (difficult, when your bathroom's not much larger than a linen closet, as ours is) but with clever storage this needn't be a trial. And with careful editing, even clutter can look fun and pretty in any home.

I bought a wonderfully inspiring book a while ago, about keeping a stylish house with children. It is entirely possible, because I know many people who've achieved it – all it takes is a bit of work and consideration. I don't want our home to become overrun with childish bits and pieces (adults have to live there too, after all) but at the same time, I wouldn't dream about tidying away Olive's existence. I want her to feel free to play and explore and learn – that's what childhood is all about, if you ask me.

If you're worried about curbing the mess, it can be a good idea to vet things carefully before they even make it through the front door. For example, we said no to the high chair that took up half the available kitchen floor space (in favour of something more streamlined), and stopped buying toys when a few designated baskets became full. But other people won't stop giving your children things – especially when it comes to birthdays and special occasions such as Christmas – so one idea is to keep a 'one in, one out' policy, where you pass something on to a friend or charity store when you receive something new. The real key is to edit – this way you'll keep the mess to a minimum, and only hold on to the things they absolutely love.

Fun in the tub

Is there anything cuter than kids at bath time? I don't know if everyone's children are the same – I imagine some hate the tub more than dogs do – but no matter how tired, sick or grumpy Olive is, she loves being in the bath. Her father has christened her legs Splashy and Kick Kick because he ends up soaked from head to toe by all the raucous messing about. We've got the whole routine down pat, and often it's the high point of the day, because she's so darn cute and happy I almost can't bear it.

Following are a few things you can make to ensure bath time is an entirely pleasurable experience for adults and children alike.

Waterproof toy basket

Make one of these useful square baskets to store all your kiddie-friendly bathroom things and keep it within easy reach of the tub. Pop it on a nearby stool or chair so you don't need to leave waterbabes alone as they splash about (always important – we've all heard how children can drown in two inches of water... best not risk it) or somewhere they can grab at things for themselves.

It really won't matter if they haul it in with them, either – that's the beauty of oilcloth. Just remember to leave it somewhere warm and dry occasionally, so it doesn't grow mould.

*Tip

You can vary the size of the basket depending on the space you have or amount of equipment you use. You might also want to make one out of sturdy cotton or hemp for other areas of the home. Small cotton versions are great for storing all manner of things, such as jewellery, keys and other odds and ends.

You will need

✳ 60 × 50 cm (24 × 19^1/$_2$ in) oilcloth in each of two different designs, and 60 × 30 cm (24 × 12 in) oilcloth in a third contrast – here I've used Cath Kidston's cute star design as well as some gingham oilcloth in blue and red

✳ Ruler

✳ Scissors

✳ Sewing machine and thread

✳ Chopsticks

Instructions

1. Cut the two larger rectangles of oilcloth in half, giving four pieces in all, each 50 × 30 cm (19^1/$_2$ × 12 in). Cut the smaller rectangle in half, giving two squares, each 30 × 30 cm (12 × 12 in).

2. Lay out all four rectangles side by side, alternating the designs.

3. Place the first and second rectangles together, right sides facing each other, and stitch together along one long edge, allowing a 6 mm (^{1}/$_4$ in) seam.

4. Keeping the alternating designs correct, join the third and fourth rectangles in the same way, then join the first edge to the fourth, creating a square-sided, open-ended tube.

5. Take one of your squares and, with right sides together, stitch it to one end of your tube, one side at a time, pivoting carefully on the needle at each corner, until you get back to the starting point.

6. Take your remaining square and sew to the other end of your tube, leaving one side open.

7. Trim the corners at each end of the tube to reduce as much bulk as possible, then turn the tube right side out, carefully pushing out the corners with chopsticks.

8. Fold under the seam allowance on the open edges and topstitch the edges together.

9. Now, push the square you have just sewn down inside the tube to meet the square at the opposite end. You are effectively, folding the tube in half, creating a lined basket.

10. Use your hands to smooth down any creases and use your fingers to create defined folds along the top rim of the basket shape you have now created. The two squares at the bottom should be aligned.

11. Hooray – you're done! Now make a matching set for other bathroom bits and pieces.

'A day's sailing' flannel

A pile of flannels is cheap and highly useful, and not just for the bath. They're also great for wiping clean small, grubby faces or mopping up spills. Turn an ordinary white one into something more fun, like this version, to evoke a lazy Sunday afternoon picnicking by the harbour.

Decorated flannels make a sweet gift for new parents or provide encouragement to small children with an aversion to bathing. Make three or four with different designs – stars, lighthouses, flowers, animals and bows all make lovely adornments – then simply fold into a nice stack and tie with a pretty ribbon.

Lie back, relax and imagine being out to sea
... what bliss

You will need

For a sailboat version:

❋ One white flannel

❋ Small pieces of fabric – beige linen, blue denim and red canvas (preferably cut from pre-loved clothes or washed fabric to ensure colours will not run in hot water)

❋ A short length of narrow ribbon

❋ Sewing machine and white thread

Instructions

1. Cut your pieces of fabric into the shapes shown in the photograph (if you're struggling to cut them freehand, you can find them in the pattern pages at the back of the book on page 242).

2. Lay them out in the bottom left-hand corner of your flannel until you're happy with the arrangement.

3. Use your sewing machine to stitch the shapes into place, reversing a few times at either end for strength. Fold under the edges if you're worried about fraying (particularly with the linen); otherwise, you can go over your lines a couple of times for strength and allow a little fraying.

4. Sew a few lines of white stitching across the blue denim for the waves.

5. Add the two short lengths of ribbon and sew into place for the mast and sail's boom.

Keeping little hands busy

Encourage your child to make a collage out of fabric scraps. Suggest a theme – say, 'Underwater' or 'The Beach' – then let them cut simple shapes, which can be glued or stitched (by you or your child) to a plain white flannel.

Include bits of ribbon and buttons on the flannel for extra texture.

Bunny ear bath hat

Who says you can't still play dress-ups in the bath?

We've been so lucky when it comes to clothes for Olive: our friends Matt and Kate have a gorgeous little girl, Ava, who is eighteen months older, and they've been kind enough to loan us all her clothes as she grows out of them. Because of this, Olive is actually kitted out in more designer clobber than I've ever owned. Yes, we are very lucky, but it means I find it hard to justify buying anything extra.

That said, I couldn't resist a red cashmere beanie I saw not long ago: I made the mistake of popping it on her head in the shop and simply had to buy it. She looks like a gumnut baby when it's on – so cute and chubby and divine, I wanted to eat her up.

That was the inspiration behind this bunny ear bath hat, which lives in her matching waterproof toy basket: I simply love a hat, and they are almost unbearably cute on children. I pop this on her in the bath and it tickles me senseless. When Olive sees me giggling, she starts too. Bath time has become even more amusing since.

You will need

✳ Tape measure

✳ Ruler

✳ Pen

✳ Oilcloth in two designs

✳ Dinner plate

✳ Scissors

✳ Sewing machine and thread

Instructions

1. Use your tape measure to measure the circumference of your little one's head and then add an extra few centimetres (³/₄ in) for the seam allowance.

2. Divide your measurement in half then rule a line across the oilcloth to this size.

3. Rule short vertical lines on either side of your horizontal line, then use the rounded edge of a plate to connect them before drawing a line with your pen around the edge.

4. Cut out the semi-circle shape, then use your first piece as a pattern to cut a second piece, right sides together. Set aside.

5. Fold your second piece of oilcloth in half, right sides together, and using the pattern on page 230, cut out two pairs of Bunny Ears (you should now have four pieces for the ears), remembering to add seam allowance around the edges.

6. Sew the Ears together in pairs around the edges, then turn each ear right side out.

7. Take one of your two semicircles of oilcloth and baste the ears to the top edge, with right sides together and raw edges matching.

8. Place the two semicircles together, right sides facing each other, and sew around the edge of the hat, leaving the bottom edge open, and reversing a few times at either end for strength.

9. Clip across the seam allowance around the curve, then turn the hat right side out. And *voilà*, you have yourself a bunny hat.

Dry off

This is when bath time can be trickiest, particularly when it comes to the cooler months. How to keep little ones warm and cosy, and stop them fussing as they dry off and get dressed? Many children will want to draw out time for play and resist the advancing inevitability of being packed off to bed.

I think the only thing for it is to make bath time an event, and as fun as humanly possible, with songs and games for getting dry, followed swiftly by a story and then bed. But this might not work for everyone. If kiddies are particularly grouchy and over it, you can be all business-like and make it clear there's to be no nonsense!

Grizzly tears may call for the bedtime story to be dropped in favour of as early a night as possible. I like to get through the whole routine quickly. Just think: once they're in peaceful slumber you can sit down, put your feet up, and perhaps indulge in a nice glass of red to wind down. Hoorah!

Love heart bath mat

Beautiful utilitarian items for everyday use are so important – particularly in the house, where they put the 'home' in 'homely'. The Italian design family Alessi knows this well – that's why their collectable household pieces are coveted around the globe (one day I will own their electric bird kettle, I will!).

Make this simple rag rug with a child out of past-it sheets, ripped up into long strips. Flannelette is particularly soft on the feet, but any old sheets worn soft by many washes will work. If you don't have any sheets that are ready to be recycled, try your local charity shop – there should be loads available, usually in fab, garish 1960s, '70s and '80s prints. Ask a small helper to braid it with you – a riot of colours will be appreciated by the youngest members of the family most of all.

You will need

✳ Dressmaker's scissors

✳ Sewing needle and thread

✳ Three strips of fabric, about 8 m ($8^3/_4$ yd) in length by 10 cm (4 in) wide for a finished rug of approximately 1 m (39 in) in diameter. You don't need 8 m ($8^3/_4$ yd) of fabric, though – cut strips from an old sheet or clothes and stitch the ends together to create the length

✳ Large safety pin

✳ Strong elastic band or hair band

Instructions

1. When you've constructed your three 8 m ($8^3/_4$ yd) long strips of fabric, hold all three ends together in a T-shape, then stitch a line in the centre where the pieces meet.

2. Use your safety pin to pin the hair band (hair bands are less likely to snap than elastic bands) to the joined end of the fabric strips. Loop the band around a door handle.

3. Start plaiting your three strips together, just as you would braid someone's hair, and move away from the door handle as the plait grows longer to keep the line taught and tension the same throughout the braid.

4. Tuck the cut or frayed edges under as you plait the fabric together. This will make the top surface of the mat smoother. Don't worry about the places where the fabric strips are joined; just roll the raw edges under.

5. When you've finished, unloop the band from the door handle and use the safety pin to secure the unstitched end, then stitch across the ends to secure them as before.

6. Take one end and place it on the floor or a table, then wind the braid around the centre, smoother side facing upwards.

7. Use your needle and thread to sew the braid together, winding it around as you go, from the inside out. Keep the braid lying on a flat surface and sew around it without pulling it, so it will sit just as flat when it's finished. Large stitches are fine, and you can either hide or make a feature of them with thread in a contrasting colour.

8. To achieve the heart shape, gently coax your winding into the shape of a heart, then stitch at the top and pull down through the centre layers to achieve the 'hills' at its top.

9. Snip off any loose threads or frayed edges.

10. Well done – it's now ready for placing underneath little feet.

'It's mine!' towel

It is unbelievably easy to edge a bath or hand towel with gorgeous fabric or pompoms, and the finished look can be so effective. If you're overwhelmed by choice when deciding on a fabric, you really can't go wrong with stripes or polka dots, and children will love them too. These towels work equally well for bath or beach, and your kids will adore being part of the process in choosing their favourite fabric as well.

For this sweet personalised towel for your little one, buy a plain white towel and some fabric in a medium weight so it can withstand a good few washes. Decent quality Egyptian cotton towels will last for years. We were given some for a wedding gift over five years ago now, use them every day, and they're still going strong.

This is one area where it's worth splurging – you'll save more money over time, and enjoy using them for much longer (who wants a cheap, scratchy towel to dry off with anyway?). And young ones will appreciate the softness of good quality towels on their delicate skin.

You will need

* One white bath towel
* Approximately 40 × 80 cm (16 × 31^1/$_2$ in) medium-weight contrasting fabric
* Sewing machine and thread
* Iron
* 20 mm-wide (^{3}/$_4$ in) woven twill tape
* Bobble-headed pins
* Needle and thread
* Buttons to match tape, for any dots (optional)

Instructions

1. Cut the hemmed edge and woven border from each end of your towel.

2. Measure the width of the towel and cut two strips of fabric, each 18 cm (7 in) wide × the width of the towel plus 2 cm (^{3}/$_4$ in) extra, for seam allowance.

3. With right sides together and raw edges matching, pin one edge of a fabric strip along one edge of your towel. The strip should extend by 1 cm (^{3}/$_8$ in) beyond the edge of the towel at each end.

4. Stitch along this seam, removing the pins as you go.

5. Using your iron, press under 1 cm (^{3}/$_8$ in) on the remaining long edge of the fabric strip.

6. With right sides together, fold the strip in half and stitch across the short end on each side.

7. Now turn the strip right side out again and press. Topstitch the folded edge neatly in place over the previous seam. You can also continue the topstitching down the short sides, if you like.

8. Repeat Steps 3–7 for the remaining strip at the other end of the towel.

9. Take your woven twill tape and start to 'write' the name of your child in loopy cursive writing across the bottom left-hand section of the towel, using your bobble-headed pins to secure the loops in place.

10. Stitch along the outer edges of each side of the tape, pivoting on the needle when you get to tight turns.

11. Use your needle and thread and buttons to sew on any dots for the letters 'j' or 'i'.

Chillybilly bathrobe

There are lots of things in life which are irresistible in miniature. Tiny shoes and boots. Baby animals. Handmade individual chocolates. A child's bathrobe – especially with a little one rugged up in it – is another of these things. I can't help smiling when I see them.

Make this bathrobe from a single bath sheet or two smaller bath towels for chilly children to rug up in before and after the tub. This one's made from two recycled towels which were beginning to fray around the edges but were otherwise still soft and faintly retro-looking (like me, you probably remember having household towels something like these yourself back in the '70s). I found them for 50 cents each at a charity store and gave them a good soak and wash before cutting them up to make this project.

The robe seems a lot more ambitious than it actually is, so here's the cheat: simply use a child's hooded sweatshirt or fleece for your pattern. If you get stuck, examine how the hoodie has been constructed and you should be able to figure out where each piece goes. The finished bathrobe will be a lot roomier than the hoodie, so this easy method will forgive non-exact measurements.

You will need

* One bath sheet or two smaller bath towels, old or new

* Cotton fabric

* Child's hoodie, to base your robe upon

* Bias binding

* Scissors

* Sewing machine and thread

* Small scrap of fabric for initial

* Sewing needle and embroidery thread

Instructions

1. Lay your bath sheet out on the table, right side down, and then place your child's hoodie over it, with the right side facing up.

2. Make sure the bottom hem of the hoodie is aligned with the bottom of the bath sheet, and leave an extra 10–15 cm (4–6 in) or more, if you want it longer, at the bottom.

3. Fold the hood and sleeves inwards, allowing the shape of the hoodie, sans hood and sleeves, to be visible.

4. You want the robe to be roomy, so give yourself a further 5 cm (2 in) of towelling around the other edges of the hoodie's body (in addition to the 10–15 cm (4–6 in) at the bottom) before cutting around the shape.

5. For the front of the robe, take the back piece which you've just cut out, and fold it in half. Place it down on the bath sheet, with the bottom hem of the pattern piece aligned with the bottom of the bath sheet.

6. From just under the neck area down, cut around the outside and flare out for several centimetres (a few inches) as you approach the middle. Continue cutting downwards now in a straight line, and then around the rest of the outline. This will give you a bit of extra fabric down the front to wrap around your child's body.

7. Repeat Steps 5–6, but with your pattern shape reversed, so that you end up with left and right sides at the front. If you have run out of terry towelling fabric along the bottom hem of the bath sheet, turn it upside down and start using the other end.

8. So, now you have the back and front of the robe. Lay the hoodie out again on the bath sheet, this time focusing on the right sleeve. Align the edge of the sleeve with the edge of the bath sheet. Now fold the bath sheet over on itself, and place the hoodie's sleeve on top to act as your guide.

9. Adding 5 cm (2 in) again, cut around the outside.

10. Repeat for the left sleeve.

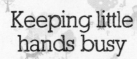

Keeping little hands busy

Your child could cut out their own initial or fabric shapes for the robe's lapel, and stitch it to the front. They could also cover any raw edges with a strip of folded-over bias binding and a simple running stitch.

11. With any remaining fabric, lay down the hood part of the hoodie. It should be made of two pieces, so fold the hoodie in half to cut out first one piece, and then the other (again leaving a further 5 cm (2 in) extra) for each side of the hood.

12. Repeat the above step with your cotton fabric – this will be the lining. Use a plain fabric if your bath sheet is patterned (as mine is) or something with a pattern if your towels or bath sheet are all the same colour.

13. Okay, the last thing you need to do before you get sewing is to cut two 8 cm-wide (3 in) strips for your robe, long enough to tie around the middle, like a belt. Just make sure they're long enough to tie in a single knot, with a bit of length to spare. My straps are each 8 × 43 cm (3 × 17 in).

14. Now, take a break for a cup of tea – it's much easier from here on in. After you've finished your tea, come back to all your cut-out pieces and lay out in correct places where they will go, once they're sewn together.

15. With right sides together, stitch each of the front panels to the back at the shoulders, allowing 1 cm ($^3/_8$ in) seams. Neaten the seams with zigzag.

16. Finish the raw edges of your ties with a narrow rolled hem or by binding the edges with bias binding.

17. With right sides together and raw edges matching, baste the ties to the side edge of each front panel, at waist level.

18. Take your sleeves, fold each one in half lengthwise and mark the centre point of the top edge with a pin – this is the point of the shoulder.

19. With right sides together and matching the pin mark to the shoulder seam, stitch each sleeve to the robe.

20. Now fold your robe with right sides together and pin one entire seam from the cuff edge of the sleeve to the bottom edge of the robe. Stitch this seam as pinned, sandwiching the raw ends of your ties in the side seam. Finish any raw edges with zigzag.

21. Repeat the last step for the other sleeve/side seam.

22. With right sides facing each other, sew the two hood pieces together around the centre seam.

23. Repeat the last step for the hood lining.

24. With right sides together, stitch the hood and hood lining to each other around the front edge. Turn hood right side out and topstitch around the front edge, about 6 mm ($1/4$ in) from the finished edge.

25. With right sides together, pin the lower edge of the towelling hood to the neck edge of the robe and stitch in place, making sure you don't catch the raw edge of the lining hood in the seam.

26. Fold under the seam allowance on the raw edge of the lining hood and topstitch in place over the previous seam line, so the raw edges of the hood are neatly enclosed.

27. Cut your child's first initial out of a small scrap of patterned fabric, then appliqué to the right side of the robe with embroidery thread Yeehah, you're done – now rug up your little one like a prize fighter!

*Tip

Try to align any hem on the robe with the hems of the towel, but use bias binding around cut edges when this becomes impossible, or simply roll under and sew a narrow hem on the edges. The only edges with new hems on my version are at the front and on the belt straps.

Jolly cute bedrooms

Inspiration to decorate a child's bedroom can come from anywhere, even if you don't read magazines or trawl through a vast number of design websites like I do. The difficulty is coming up with one concept! You certainly don't need to make a significant investment of time or money to create a space they will adore. Often, very few changes or additions can completely change the look and feel of a room, so choose your basic furniture wisely and add embellishments to create its unique character, updating the theme often and playing with paint and soft furnishings rather than investing in key pieces more than once. This formula will carry you well throughout the years, and not just in this area of the home.

I like the idea of the constantly evolving room, and never more so than when it comes to bedrooms for children. Because, although children usually have places within and outside the home where they are given free reign to play, the bedroom is the only place they will feel is really their own, surrounded by all their favourite things. As the years pass, our kids go through so many phases and changing likes and dislikes. Embrace each new stage afresh and enjoy helping them navigate their way through each set of challenges, making their room a stage set for the drama of their lives, or dreamy and soothing, if you think they could do with fewer distractions. Consider it an honour if they appreciate your ideas and allow you to choose things to express their personality as they grow older, or take them on shopping trips to markets and second-hand stores where they can decide (with a little guidance) on their own most favourite additions. This is not about spoiling them, but listening to their needs. All of us should be surrounded by beauty or, at least, items that 'speak' to us and reflect our individuality. Our children are no different, and may even need this more than we do in the impressionable early years.

Here are some ideas for making your child's space both special and distinctive, and tailored to include all the things they treasure most.

Très jolie adornments

While I'm all for keeping a streamlined home – remember my favourite adage: if you don't love it or use it, get rid of it – and therefore not fond of dust-collectors (that is, useless fripperies) sometimes a knitted doughnut or miniature tea-set just wins me over, and I can't resist buying it on the spot. Never mind that it'll be a while before Olive's old enough to appreciate it. In this respect, online shopping sites can be particularly dangerous… the power of the 'click to buy' can be hard to resist.

This chapter is all about (kind of) useful things that are lots of fun also, and should amuse you and your little ones for hours on end, in either the making or enjoying of them. Let them inspire a sense of personal achievement as well – if only because you sourced and matched all the materials, not to mention constructed them yourself from scratch. Hurrah for resourceful Crafty Minxes and their crafty poppets!

Falling petals mobile

There's something very soothing about watching a mobile bob and turn slightly with the breeze, but it's not just babies who love them. Certain chic, upmarket homewares boutiques stock mobiles made specifically for grown-ups, which are covetable indeed, but come with grown-up-sized price tags attached. James and I fell in love with a Miro-esque piece recently, but he almost fainted when we saw the price tag of $1500. It prompted me to attempt making my own and I have to say, I now prefer mine!

This mobile is very simple to construct and will be appreciated by older children and kidults, too.

Keeping little hands busy

A child who can handle scissors would love to help by cutting the petal shapes. If they find heavyweight fabric too difficult to handle, why not let them create their very own mobile by providing finer fabric scraps for them to cut instead.

These petals may flop a little, but the effect will still be very pretty. Another option is for them to simply tie scraps onto lengths of string, and watch them gently twist and turn.

You will need

* Paper
* Pencil
* Scissors
* Small scraps heavyweight cotton or canvas fabric
* Small scraps floral cotton fabrics
* Two wire coat hangers (the kind dry-cleaners use)
* Tin snips
* 25 mm-wide (1 in) bias binding
* Sewing machine and thread
* Embroidery needle and thread
* Five small buttons

Instructions

1. Use the pattern on page 235 to trace and cut 15 double petal shapes from your heavyweight cotton, and 15 from a variety of different floral cotton scraps.

2. Set your machine to zigzag and, placing a floral fabric petal on top of a heavyweight cotton petal, wrong sides together, sew around the outer edges of the double petals. Repeat for all 15 double petals.

3. Take each petal and pinch the middle edges together. Change the setting on your machine to a straight stitch, and stitch the pinched edges together in a short line, reversing a few times to stop stitching from coming apart. Repeat for all petals and set them aside.

4. Use your tin snips to cut away the bottom straight edge of each wire coat hanger, making one slightly shorter than the other.

5. Cut two pieces of bias binding, about 1 cm (³/8 in) longer than each piece of wire. Fold the binding in half lengthwise, wrong sides together and sew the long edges and one short end together, stitching close to the edge. Pop your wire into each length of binding, and use a needle and thread to sew the open ends closed.

6. Thread your embroidery needle with a long length of thread and tie a knot at the end. Anchor the knot in the end of one piece of bias-covered wire, then take the needle through the middle of one of your petals. Tie a knot underneath the petal when you are satisfied with where it's sitting along the piece of thread, and continue in this way until you've threaded on three petals.

7. When you have three petals on the thread, stitch a small button to the centre of the bottom petal to act as a weight.

8. Repeat Steps 6 and 7 until you have threaded three petals (and a button) to each end of both bias-covered wires.

9. Thread another three petals and a button onto the middle of the longer length of wire.

10. Use more embroidery thread to suspend the longer wire below the shorter wire in the middle.

11. Attach a thinner cotton hanging thread to the middle of the upper wire, then suspend your mobile from a hook in the ceiling and watch it turn lazily all day long.

Super door snake

Despite living through several northern hemisphere winters, I've never been as cold for sustained periods of time as I have here in Sydney. Actually, that's not true: once I was living in a rambling old terrace in London's Clapham South when it was snowing outside and the boiler broke. I had to sleep in several layers of clothing, my dressing gown and under a couple of towels as well as my duvet for a couple of nights. The saner people in the household disappeared off to friends' houses until it was fixed, while I came down with bronchitis. But that's the exception!

At least in chillier climes, central heating, insulation and double-glazing are installed pretty much everywhere. Here, many of us perpetuate the myth that it doesn't actually get cold, and end up almost freezing to death for those few really icy weeks each winter. Make one of these door snakes to stop chilly breezes creeping under wee ones' doors, or to keep the heat in – especially important if you have a freezing old Victorian-era home like we do, with lots of inch-sized gaps around the windows and door frames to let in the howling wind.

These are so simple to make, little ones can easily construct them on their own. Just give them a large, not-too-sharp needle and thread to make one by hand rather than on the machine, but create an inner layer so the sand or rice doesn't fall out.

*Tip

When you're buying or recycling fabric for this project, try choosing one with a pattern that works for the finished size of 8 cm (3 in) high, as with this bird-printed design, to show off the design to full effect.

You will need

✳ A piece of fairly sturdy fabric, 18 × 90 cm (7 × 35½ in)

✳ Sewing machine and thread, *or* large sewing needle and wool thread

✳ Sand or rice

Instructions

1. Take your piece of material and fold it in half lengthwise, right sides together, so it measures 9 × 90 cm (3½ × 35½ in).

2. Allowing a 1 cm (³⁄₈ in) seam, sew along one long side and across one short end with small firm stitches, leaving remaining short end open.

3. To make a boxed corner on the end, pinch a triangle on each corner of the stitched short side and stitch across the triangle, about 3 cm (1¼ in) down from the apex. Trim back excess fabric.

4. You now have a long tube with a squarish end. Turn it right side out and fill with sand or rice.

5. To box the remaining corner, fold in the seam allowance on the open end and stitch the edges together, but leave about 2.5 cm (1 in) unstitched at each end. Pinch the unstitched section at right angles to the stitched section and topstitch across the edges. Repeat on the opposite unstitched section.

6. Place against the door and enjoy being toasty (or at least, a little less cold).

Keeping little hands busy

If a young helper is going to make one of these, chances are their stitches are going to be too big to keep in the filling. Make a calico version on the machine that will fit inside the child's carefully stitched outer cover – a sense of achievement all round!

Fabric collage wall hangings

These are so simple to make I'm almost embarrassed to list them as a project, but I've seen the same concept in so many chichi children's stores for up to $100 a pop, I felt compelled to share its simplicity with the novice crafter. This is a perfect project for children, requiring very little time and effort for an immensely satisfying end result.

Collect favourite pieces of fabric to use for these. Images of people or animals look wonderful stitched against a plain backdrop, or can be layered over an equally distinctive fabric for a 'more is more' effect. Or cut patterned fabric into a recognisable shape for the feature. Staple your finished effort to a wooden frame, or stretch it within an embroidery hoop before hanging on the wall.

*Tip

Another idea is to simply buy very cheap, pre-made canvases from a two-dollar shop and cover them with your artfully arrayed fabric. This works just as well and is a cheaper alternative if you plan to create an entire collection of collage wall hangings.

You will need

* Wooden canvas stretcher, available from an art supplies store, or embroidery hoop, available from a crafts store

* Hammer

* Background fabric to fit the frame (remember to leave a bit extra on each side to wrap around and behind frame)

* Pieces of fabric to feature: either printed with an animal design or to cut shapes

* Appliqué glue

* Embroidery needle and thread

* Staple gun

* Two small screw-in eye hooks

* Hanging wire

* Pliers

Instructions

1. Slot all four sides of the wooden stretcher together and use the hammer to tap into place.

2. Lay out your background fabric and arrange the smaller pieces you will appliqué to the front in the correct spots.

3. Use a little appliqué glue to fix the pieces, then sew around the edges in a running stitch with your embroidery thread. (The final piece won't need to go through the wash, so there's no need to overly protect the edges of the smaller pieces of fabric from fraying with pinking shears.)

4. Lay your fabric face down, and place the frame over it.

5. Fold the edges of the fabric over the frame and staple into place, carefully folding the edges under so they sit as flat as possible. (If you're using an embroidery hoop to frame your work, just slide the larger hoop into place and tighten screws.)

6. Use your hammer to tap the eye hooks slightly into the back of the frame on either side.

7. Screw eye hooks in, then wrap hanging wire to fit from one hook to the other, twisting around the edges and cutting off any excess with your pliers.

8. Hang above a child's bed or even better, create a number in different sizes and display together on the wall in your own gallery show.

Quiet time in my special space

I've already expressed how important I think it is for children to have quiet time by themselves, and the space to enjoy it. Time to contemplate, ruminate... even to get thoroughly bored, because that's when inspiration often strikes.

As an energetic and outgoing child who was also very bookish, I remember I needed time on my own to recharge my batteries when I was little – I still do. Leaving kids alone once in a while encourages them to be independent, and shows them we trust them to behave appropriately when left to their own devices. We know ourselves if we're on the go all the time that we relish such moments of solitude, and tend to look forward to them. Why fill every moment of every day with activity? Peace is so necessary at times, too, for our good health and wellbeing.

The following few projects are designed for your little one's relaxation: an accessory to get them started on their crafty journey, and a couple of things comfy enough to curl up against while reading, thinking or dropping off to sleep. Enjoy!

Heart-shaped pincushion

Not all children enjoy sewing, but if your little ones have clamoured to be involved with your sewing projects in the past, this is the perfect thing to get them started. The heart-shaped pincushion could become their first 'accessory', once they're old enough to get stuck into pins (no pun intended).

And the elastic band means they can wear it on their wrists (or just wear it, full stop), even when they're not being crafty.

Win their hearts with a simple craft project or three

You will need

✳ Small swatch of red polka dot fabric

✳ Elastic

✳ Scissors

✳ Needle and thread

✳ Chopstick

✳ Fabric scraps/fibrefill

✳ A spanking-new pack of pearly bobble-headed pins

Instructions

1. Fold your fabric in half, right sides together.

2. Using the outline on page 242, trace and cut a pair of Hearts from your folded fabric, adding 6 mm ($^1/_4$ in) seam allowance all round when cutting. The traced line will be your stitching line.

3. With right sides together, sew the hearts to each other around the traced stitching line with backstitch, leaving a 5 cm (2 in) opening in a straight section of the seam.

4. Carefully clip across the seam allowance on the curves to ensure that the seam will sit flat, without puckers.

5. Turn the heart right side out, using the chopstick to poke out the shape completely.

6. Stuff with fibrefill or old fabric scraps (or a mixture of both to avoid it looking too lumpy), then fold in the seam allowance on the unfinished edges inwards and neatly slipstitch the opening closed.

7. Take the elastic and measure it in a loop around your child's wrist, stretching a little – you want it to be stretched (but not so much so that you'll cut off the circulation to their hands!).

8. Stitch the ends of the elastic into a loop, then sew the loop to the back of your padded heart shape.

9. Stick in your pack of bobble-headed pins... how sweet is that?

Fun-sized beanbag

You've got to love a beanbag. What says childish fun more than slouching about on a bag of beans? Or even pitching into one after a running jump? This is the mini version for wee ones which won't take up too much space, but still provides a comfy resting place. Drag it out to the living room for movie days, served with a huge bowl of freshly made popcorn, or leave little ones alone to read on wet afternoons.

*Tip

The cover of a child's beanbag needs to take a lot of wear and tear. They wriggle and squirm and jump on it, not to mention the Vegemite hands and occasional accident. Choose a good, sturdy fabric that is going to survive repeated washes such as a lovely upholstery fabric, like this Florence Broadhurst running horses print.

You will need

∗ About 2 m (2¹/₄ yd) sturdy canvas fabric, or a number of different fabrics to make 4 triangle panels, each 50 × 80 cm (20 × 31¹/₂ in), one 50 cm (20 in) square and one 10 cm (4 in) square.

∗ Same amount calico or fabric scraps, for lining

∗ 60 cm (24 in) zipper

∗ Sewing machine and thread

∗ Measuring tape

∗ Ruler

∗ Scissors

∗ Sewing machine and thread

∗ Polystyrene bean bag beans

∗ Needle and thread

Instructions

1. Lay calico out on the floor or table, and use your tape, ruler and chalk to measure and draw a triangle that is 50 cm (20 in) across the base and 80 cm (31¹/₂ in) high from base to apex.

2. Cut out the triangle with your scissors.

3. Fold down the apex until the top folded edge measures 10 cm (4 in) from side to side. Press the fold line with your fingers to mark it, then open out the fabric again and cut off the top of the triangle along the marked line. The shape you now have is a triangle with the top lopped off – a bit like a volcano.

4. Use this piece as a pattern to cut three more 'volcano' pieces from calico, and four 'volcano' pieces from coloured fabric – eight pieces in all, including your original pattern piece (four calico pieces for the lining, and four coloured pieces for the outer bean bag).

5. You also need to measure and cut one 50 cm (20 in) square from both printed fabric and calico, and one 10 cm (4 in) square from both printed fabric and calico.

6. Lay two of your calico triangles, right sides together and, allowing a 1.5 cm (⁵/₈ in) seam, stitch together from top to bottom along one side edge.

7. Add the two remaining calico triangles in the same fashion, until all four are sewn together along the longer edges.

8. With right sides together, join the first triangle to the last along the remaining long edges to make one pyramid-shaped piece, but leave a 20 cm (8 in) opening in the middle of the seam (for inserting the beans).

9. Take your smaller calico square and, with right sides together, pin the edges to the squared-off top edges of your pyramid, then stitch as pinned.

10. Take your larger calico square, and follow the same instructions for the bottom of the bag's lining.

11. Turn the lining bag right side out through the opening you left, and set it aside.

12. Follow Steps 6–8 for the bean bag's outer case, but in Step 8, leave an opening large enough to fit your zip in the last seam.

13. Insert the zip into the opening.

14. Leaving the zip slightly open, follow Steps 9 and 10 to add the top and bottom squares to your outer case.

15. Turn the case right side out through the zip opening.

16. Fill the inner lining with your polystyrene beans. It's a good idea to do this in a dry bath with the plug in to avoid spilling beans everywhere. Fill the bag firmly, but not so tight that it won't accommodate the weight of a small, nestling body.

17. When you're done, fold under the seam allowance on the opening edges and use the needle and thread to sew the opening closed with small, firm stitches.

18. Pop the lining bag inside the cover, zip it up and there you have it: one finished bean bag.

Keeping little hands busy

It's not a good idea to let little ones near the polystyrene beans as they are very hard to contain and could be inhaled. But why not get them cutting, stitching and decorating felt or fabric squares that can be used to decorate their bean bags?

Woolly lapped-back cushion

This is a wonderful way to recycle old jumpers, turning them into a very precious cushion your child could hold onto for life. Mix and match colours judiciously, such as these gelati-inspired ones which go so well together (pistachio, strawberry and vanilla – *yum*) to pick up the tones in their bedroom.

If you don't have the right shades of old, holey jumpers already sitting in the crafts cupboard, make a trip to your local charity store or flea market to find them. Don't forget to give jumpers a good wash in a gorgeously-scented wool wash before cutting up, pulling them into shape and leaving out of the sun somewhere warm to dry. To kill off any moth eggs, pop in a plastic bag, tie a knot and store in the freezer for 24 hours before washing.

Snuggle into this cosy cushion, made from a selection of favourite old jumpers

You will need

✳ Three jumpers (preferably of a similar thickness of yarn)

✳ 50 cm (20 in) square cushion insert

✳ Ruler

✳ Wool, to use as thread

✳ Large wool needle for hand-stitching

✳ Large vintage button

Instructions

1. Measure and cut four 13.5 cm ($5^1/_4$ in) squares from the front of your jumpers for the front of your cushion.

2. With right sides together, sew the four patches to each other in a 2 × 2 block, using backstitch with your wool thread, allowing a 6 mm ($^1/_4$ in) seam and making sure the weave is all running in the same direction.

3. Measure and cut a 50 cm (20 in) wide by 40 cm (16 in) high rectangle from the back of one jumper, measuring from the finished bottom edge up. Measure and cut another 50 cm (20 in) wide by 25 cm (10 in) high strip from the back of another jumper, again measuring from the bottom edge.

4. Place your patchwork cushion front on the table, with the right side facing up.

5. Lay your backing pieces on top, wrong side up, lapping the finished edge of the larger piece under the finished edge of the smaller piece until the backing square is the same size as the front.

6. Put a couple of basting stitches in each side to hold the lapped edges together while you sew.

7. Now, with right sides facing each other, stitch the front of the cushion to the lapped back around all four edges, using wool thread and backstitch, as before.

8. Turn the cover right side out and pop in the cushion insert, tucking it under the lapped back like a pillowcase... almost done.

9. Take your needle and wool thread and place your large vintage button at the centre front of your cushion. Fix in place by sewing through the cushion from front to back and tying off firmly, which will give you a lovely, plump, Chesterfield sofa effect.

10. Now – cuddle up and dream.

'To sleep, perchance to dream...'

No-one in my family is, or has ever been, one to hang around in bed. We're very much morning people who rise once we're awake – except on the weekend, when I do love to take the papers and my first tea of the day propped up against fluffy pillows... as long as I still have time to make the markets well before the Madding Crowd. We find it hard to lay about when there are things to be done, which is always, really. Even as a girl, I was up at 5 am most mornings, and made a huge song and dance about being put to bed each night.

It can be quite a mission getting wee ones to go down without a fight in the evening. Or for an afternoon nap, for that matter. I've come to the conclusion that, for the Dousts at least, bed has to be made as attractive as possible a place to spend time in, otherwise we worry we're missing out on something and consequently will not fall asleep.

I have made the following things to distract Olive from the fact I'm popping her to bed. It doesn't always work, but I've mastered the deft skill of the switcheroo: one stuffed toy for one disappearing Mummy. Playtime on the living room floor in exchange for one brightly-patterned quilt in the cot. Don't underestimate the art of distraction; it can be quite handy under the circumstances.

Hand-stitched silk eiderdown

I've said before I don't have the patience for making quilts and once it was indeed the case, but when I eventually sat down to try, I realised they're not actually so difficult after all. You don't need to make them as complex as some of those granny versions with hundreds of pieces in different shapes – keep it easy, and you'll be surprised how effective, and still very smart, the finished product looks. I think simple's much more chic, anyway. I've seen some crazy quilt patterns which must have been phenomenally difficult to construct, but which make me feel like I'm having a migraine just to look at them.

This quilt – actually more along the lines of an eiderdown – is a doddle because you don't even need to muck about with patchworking. If you *do* want to play with the top part, this is the perfect opportunity to experiment with the concept of high and low: mix some recycled fabric from a child's favourite shirt or dress they've grown out of, say, with some stylish screen-printed linen from Japan or soft, unpatterned cotton.

But here, I've simply used one gorgeous swathe of silk satin for the entire casing. And rather than fiddling about stitching through the batting on the machine, which can be especially difficult on slippery fabric, I've used a simple running stitch, and completed it by hand. Don't you think it looks rather expensive?

✳Tip

If you want an especially fluffy quilt, use two layers of wool batting, or look for other high-loft battings, preferably made from natural fibre.

You will need

✳ 3 m × 112 cm-wide ($3^1/_4$ yd × 44 in) silk satin

✳ 150 × 112 cm ($58^1/_2$ × 44 in) wool batting

✳ Sewing machine and thread

✳ Quilting ruler

✳ Dressmaker's pencil

✳ Embroidery needle and thread

Instructions

1. Cut your silk in half crosswise, giving two pieces, each 150 × 112 cm ($58^1/_2$ × 44 in).

2. Lay your silk rectangles, on a flat surface, right sides together or, if like mine, your fabric is gorgeous on the wrong side, use one piece on the 'wrong' side for the backing.

3. Lay the batting on top of the silk rectangles and pin together around the edges, through all three layers.

4. Allowing a 1 cm ($^3/_8$ in) seam, stitch around the edges of the quilt, leaving a 25 cm opening in one short edge.

5. To reduce bulk, carefully trim the seam allowance of the batting only close to the seam line. Clip off the excess fabric on the corners.

6. Turn your quilt right side out, then fold in the seam allowance on the opening edges and slipstitch the opening closed.

7. Use your quilting ruler and dressmaker's pencil to draw lines on the top of the quilt, creating a grid of 20 cm (8 in) squares over the entire top of the quilt. (If your fabric is a different size to mine, you might want to use a calculator to work out how large each square should be to get an even number of them across your quilt top.)

8. Now use your embroidery needle and thread to sew a running stitch along all the lines.

9. When you're done, dust off the chalk lines by hand or with a damp cloth, and throw the quilt over the end of your little one's bed.

Hootie the Owl softie

I've got a bit of a thing for owls: they're so wise and majestic-looking. My mother- and father-in-law's old dairy farm has one living in the eaves of the barn where we were married. We didn't disturb his nest, even when the DJ set up rather near it to play at our reception, although I was always itching to take a closer look. Thankfully, we didn't scare him off with all the 1960s and '70s tunes we were playing into the wee hours. I think he must be a Rolling Stones fan (either that, or he was out hunting anyway).

Make this sturdy softie from any remnant or second-hand fabric you have lying about. Here, I've used such diverse pieces as an old pair of my husband's jeans, a garish '70s pillowcase, an old '60s trench (that's the big button you see acting as one of his eyes), a woollen blanket and some very small remnants of soft hemp.

Owls are nocturnal creatures, so rest assured they'll be watching over your little one as they sleep

Keeping little hands busy

An older child could help with the stuffing and sew on the button eyes with a little guidance. If that's proving a challenge, why not provide a large needle and thread, a piece of fabric and lots of buttons and start with a button-sewing lesson – a useful skill for life!

You will need

* Scraps of fabric
* Two large buttons (they don't need to match)
* Scissors
* Sewing machine and thread
* Needle and thread
* Chopstick
* Polyester fibrefill

Instructions

1. Lay out your scraps of fabric and trace and cut out the shapes on page 236, cutting two Owl shapes and four Wings (adding 6 mm ($1/4$ in) seam allowance), and one Eye, one Beak and one Tummy (without seam allowance).

2. Set your machine to a small zigzag stitch and then sew around the edges of the Tummy, Eye and Beak shapes, appliquéing them to the front of the Owl shape.

3. Sew on the button eyes with a nice contrasting thread.

4. Set your machine back to a straight stitch and, with right sides together and allowing a 6 mm ($1/4$ in) seam, sew around the outside edges of the Wing pairs, leaving an opening of about 3 cm ($1 1/4$ in) where the wings attach to the body.

5. Clip across the seam allowance on any curves and turn right side out, poking out the shape carefully with the chopstick before filling very lightly with polyfill.

6. Machine-stitch over the wings, as shown on the pattern piece, to delineate the flight feathers.

7. With right sides together and raw edges matching, baste the wings to each side of the Owl front.

8. Place the two Owl shapes together, right sides facing each other, machine-stitch around the edges with small, firm stitches, leaving about 8 cm (3 in) open at the base.

9. Clip any curves, then turn right side out and use the chopstick again to poke out all the corners. Stuff with polyfill.

10. Stitch the opening closed by hand with needle and thread.

11. You're done. Whoo! Whoo!

'My name is...' pillowcase

I love personalising children's gifts. It's a bit naff having your name or initials plastered all over your belongings when you're a grown-up, but it looks so cute on things for kids. This is such a simple idea, but looks very effective when you combine a variety of luscious fabrics against white. Decorate further with bright embroidery thread in contrasting colours.

Use this idea on a whole range of things rather than just a pillowcase, if you like. Why not personalise a set of curtains, or a duvet cover, or even pop their name or initials on a fabric canvas to hang above the bed? And these suggestions make great gifts for your children's friends also – a personalised pillowcase will take no time to whip up on a pre-bought case and is likely to be the favourite at any birthday party, especially with Mum and Dad who will appreciate the handmade element.

You will need

* One plain white pillowcase

* Smallish scraps of patterned or coloured cotton fabric, for the letters

* Dressmaker's chalk

* Pinking shears

* Bobble-headed pins

* Sewing machine and thread

Instructions

1. Use dressmaker's chalk to draw your child's name or initials on the scraps of fabric.

2. Cut out with your pinking shears.

3. Centre the letters on the front of your pillowcase and use the pins to hold them in place while you baste them down with a few big stitches.

4. Set your sewing machine to a straight stitch and sew around the outside of the letters to appliqué them to the pillowcase. Make sure you first pull the back of the pillowcase aside – you don't want to stitch both sides together... it'll be very difficult to get your pillow in if you do!

5. Finish with embroidery thread around the outsides of the letters in a running stitch, using contrasting colours to highlight the letters.

6. Stuff with a plump pillow and prop against your child's bedhead – they will love it.

Keeping little hands busy

Spend time selecting favourite fabrics with your child for their very own pillowcase – they'll feel extra clever coming up with their own combination. Help them affix their name to the front also with a simple running stitch.

Glossary

✳ **Casing** — A wide double hem that is used to thread ribbon or elastic through.

✳ **Clip across the corner** — When you sew around a 90-degree corner, such as on a cushion cover, before turning the piece right side out, trim diagonally across each corner, close to the stitching. This reduces the bulk of fabric in the corner so that when you turn the piece right side out, your corners form neat points.

✳ **Clip the curves** — When you sew a seam around a curve, before you turn the item right side out, carefully make small snips across the seam allowance towards your stitching. Take great care not to actually snip into the stitching itself. Make these snips at 1–2 cm (1/2–3/4 in) intervals. When you turn the item right side out, the curved seam will sit nice and flat, without puckers.

✳ **Double hem** — Turn the raw edge of your fabric to the wrong side – an iron is handy for doing this – then turn under the folded edge again and stitch along the inner edge. This creates a neat hem that completely encloses the raw edge.

✳ **Double-sided appliqué webbing** — A wonderful adhesive-backed paper that enables you to cut and adhere appliqué shapes to fabric. It also seals the raw edges of the shapes, making fraying less of a problem. The only thing you need to remember is that the finished shapes will be mirror-images of the way they were traced — so if you're using letters, you need to trace them back-to-front.

✳ **French seam** — This seam is stitched in two stages. First, lay your pieces of fabric together with the wrong sides facing each other. Stitch a narrow seam around the edges. Now turn the piece inside out, so the right sides are now facing each other. Use your iron to press the seamed edges nice and flat. Stitch around the edges again, allowing a slightly wider seam allowance than before. Turn the item right side out and press again. A French seam totally encloses the raw edges of your fabric so that no fraying can occur. It is ideal for delicate fabrics, those that fray badly or for items that need frequent washing.

✳ Interfacing — A woven or non-woven fabric that is used to reinforce fabric, giving it more strength or body. It comes in a variety of thicknesses and is also available in a fusible version, which is ironed in place on the wrong side of your fabric.

✳ Machine-baste — Change the stitch length on your machine to the longest stitch available and stitch pieces together to hold them until you do the final stitching. It's the same as tacking by hand.

✳ Reverse at each end — When you sew a seam on the machine, you need to secure the threads so that the seam does not unravel. You can do this by reversing back and forth at each end of the seam. You can also pull the bobbin thread through to the front and tie off both threads by hand.

✳ Right sides together — Place your pieces together so that the outside or patterned sides are facing inwards towards each other, and the wrong sides are facing out.

✳ Seam allowance — The measurement that you need to add to the edges of your fabric when cutting to allow for stitching the seams. It can vary from 5 mm to 2 cm (1/4 in to 3/4 in), depending on the fabric itself and the nature of your project. You do not need to add seam allowance to edges that will be finished with bias binding.

✳ Topstitch — A line of stitching done on the right side of the fabric. It can be used both decoratively and to add strength to seams and edges.

✳ Zipper foot — A special narrow foot for your sewing machine that allows you to sew close to the edge of the zipper teeth.

Patterns

Cupcake hair clip

(actual size)

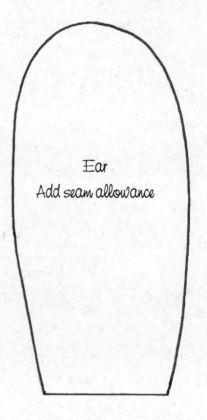

Ear
Add seam allowance

Bunny ear bath hat

Kitchen lovebirds mobile

(actual size)